FAMILY ADVENTURE GUIDE™

WISCONSIN

WISCONSIN

FAMILY ADVENTURE GUIDE™

by

MARTIN HINTZ AND
STEPHEN V. HINTZ

A VOYAGER BOOK

The
Globe
Pequot
Press

OLD SAYBROOK, CONNECTICUT

Library of Congress Cataloging-in-Publication Data
Hintz, Martin
   Family adventure guide : Wisconsin / by Martin Hintz and Stephen
V. Hintz. — 1st ed.
      p. cm. — (Family adventure guide series)
   "A voyager book."
   Includes index.
   ISBN 1-56440-615-6
      1. Wisconsin—Guidebooks. 2. Family recreation—Wisconsin—
Guidebooks. I. Hintz, Stephen V. II. Title. III. Series.
F579.3.H55   1995   95-13044
917.7504'43—dc20   CIP

Manufactured in the United States of America
First Edition/First Printing

To the family, again . . . travelers all

WISCONSIN

Hayward

NORTH–NORTHWEST

51

Rhinelander

8

Lady Smith

8

NORTH–NORTHEAST

Wausau

94

Eau Claire

SOUTHWEST

Green Bay

Wisconsin Rapids

51

Oshkosh

90

41

La Crosse

90

CENTRAL

SOUTHEAST

94

Madison

Milwaukee

Prairie
du Chien

94

90

41

Kenosha

CONTENTS

ACKNOWLEDGMENTS

The authors would like to thank all the Wisconsinites whose professionalism and hospitality laid the groundwork for this book over the years: from the tour guides to the trolley operators, from hotelkeepers to campground owners, from waitresses to game park managers. Their love of Wisconsin was always obvious, making our researching and writing about all these attractions a pleasant task.

Special thanks are extended to the staff of the Wisconsin Division of Tourism; to Gary Knowles; to travel writer Don Davis, whose state-sponsored Wisconsin Auto Tours Guide was an invaluable resource; and to Heather Demers, for her assistance in reviewing and indexing the manuscript.

INTRODUCTION

"On Wisconsin, on Wisconsin"—the strains of the university's fight song echo from the northern pine glades rimming Lake Superior to the rolling farm fields of the Swiss-like southern counties. Wisconsin is a state for "getting it on," whether your family fare consists of festivals, baseball, waterslides, hiking, ballet, or beaches. There is a delightful menu of attractions and events from which to choose fun for all seasons.

The Badger State celebrates heartily, with plenty of down-home zest, all of which takes advantage of geography, ethnic heritage, contemporary lifestyles, and person-made wonders. You can tour a House on the Rock, sit in the mouth of a giant muskie (a statue, of course), climb into a kettle (a depression in the ground caused by melting glacial ice), take in a rainbow of cultures from Haitian to Hmong, and generally kick back and enjoy.

The state is made for families looking for the offbeat, as well as the traditional. You want to waterslide? Wisconsin has 'em. You want to drive? The state has 108,000 miles of roads to meander. You want to fish? Try angling in Lake Michigan off Algoma, which is the Trout and Salmon Capital of the state, or dipping a line into a stream near Birchwood, the Bluegill Capital of the state.

How about a farm breakfast? The Kostuch Farm near Amherst Junction in Portage County even offers a milk-drinking contest to folks who regularly turn out for dawn dining on the second Saturday of each June. The Hopp Family Farm near Waupaca County's Clintonville serves up a monster omelette made from twenty-two dozen home-produced eggs that same weekend. The Wisconsin Milk Marketing Board (608–836–

8820) has listings of more breakfasts, featuring good, down-home chow and plenty of cow juice.

No one runs out of activities in Wisconsin. There is always more . . . and still more. Try these as a sampling of what you will find in Wisconsin:

❋ World Concertina Congress Jamboree Festival, Allenton. Squeezebox enthusiasts from around the world attend this melodic fest early each September at Veterans Memorial Park. They listen to concertina concerts, trade instruments, and generally talk shop. Call (414) 629–5232.

❋ Great River Traditional Music and Crafts Festival, La Crosse. Musicians, artists, and craftspeople from around the Midwest share in the folk music, dancing, and storytelling at this annual event held the first weekend in September. Noted performers include such entertainers as Peter Ostruschko, Dean McGraw, Chuck Suchy, Garnet Rodgers, and Eileen McCann. There's also a juried art show with more than fifty exhibitors, along with workshops and kids' activities. Call (608) 785–1434.

❋ U.S. Watermelon Seed-Spitting & Speed-Eating Championship, Pardeeville. Here's a chance to dig into delicious Wisconsin-grown watermelon, let the juice dribble down your chin, and act like a kid again. Anybody can enter the competitions by signing in at the registration desk as the events begin. Winners receive a mug trophy. The seed-spitting has been held annually the second Sunday in September since 1972; call (608) 429–2873 for more information. Records to beat include the champion adult spit of 61 feet, 3 inches and the junior champ spit of 32 feet, 2½ inches (set by an eight-year-old).

❋ Bicycling. This almost seems to be the state's favorite outdoor sport, with a free bike map outlining hundreds of miles of trails available from the Wisconsin Division of Tourism, 123 West Washington Avenue, Box 7606, Madison 53707. Call (800) 432–TRIP. Try the Elroy-Sparta Trail, a 33-mile former railroad bed that carries bikers through wooded valleys and small towns. Parts of the trail go through tunnels. There are campgrounds along the way. Call (608) 463-7109. Another hot spot for cyclists is the Great River Trail: Following the shore of the Mississippi River, this trail traces a 22½-mile path from Onalaska north through Trempealeau and Perrot state parks to the Trempealeau National Wildlife Refuge. Stand at the edge of 500-foot-high bluffs over the river for great views of the 6,000-acre preserve. American bald eagles are in abundance, attracting bird lovers from around the country. Call (608) 534-6409.

☀ Antiques and Arts. From urban art fairs to backcountry woodcarving exhibitions, Wisconsin has numerous opportunities to browse and shop for antiques and arts. Here are two places to find bargains, especially in old toys. First there is the Columbus Antique Mall and Museum (414-623-1992 or 800-642-1492) where 130 dealers offer their wares. The museum also contains more than 2,000 artifacts from the 1893 Columbian World Exposition in Chicago. Then there is the Northwoods Antique Show and Sale in Eagle River, with jewelry, wicker furniture, glassware, quilts, china, pottery, and folk art.

Families visiting Wisconsin can hike into the deep woods, experience hot-air balloon rides, charter-fish on Lake Michigan, attend a theatrical performance, or simply marvel at the views. Your choice, your time.

Make the best of it. And have lots—loads, tons, multitudinous amounts—of fun while doing it. We have.

The prices and rates listed in this guidebook were confirmed at press time. We recommend, however, that you call establishments before traveling to obtain current information.

51
45
Eagle River
Rhinelander
8
Pembine
Laona
Ephraim
45
Mountain
Wausau
Shawano
Clintonville
Sturgeon Bay
Iola
57
Wautoma
New London
Seymour
Green Bay
10
De Pere
Manawa
41
Waupaca
43
Two Rivers
Oshkosh
Manitowoc
Ripon
Elkhart
Green Lake
Lake
Fond du Lac
Greenbush
Kohler
Sheboygan
Horicon
Dundee

North-Northeast

NORTH-NORTHEAST

The cry of a loon, the rush of waterfalls, the perfume of towering pines, happy Holsteins, the turmoil of traffic, the slap of Lake Michigan waves upon the shore: Wisconsin's north and northeast region is a composite of the rural, the wild, and the urban. From its border with Michigan's upper peninsula to the expanding suburbs of greater Milwaukee, this awesome stretch of countryside piles attraction on attraction for the benefit of meandering families.

Kids will go nuts on the trails and theme parks; older folks will love the museums. And everyone, of course, knows that the best food in the state is found here (don't let the other parts of Wisconsin hear about that!).

This hunk of northern and northeastern Wisconsin has a touch of Canada's vast forestland, a bit of the Cape Cod ocean feel, a lively metropolitan drama scene, pro football, train museums, and just plain fun. No one can go wrong hoofing the hiking trails, biking abandoned rail grades, and discovering that in the meantime, yes, there are fine arts festivals and galleries even out here.

CLINTONVILLE

Anyone into muscle machines will love meandering through the **Four-Wheel Drive Museum** (715–823–2141) in Clintonville, where the first four-by-four was engineered in 1908. Built to get through the area's thick forestlands, whether in mud or snow, the original vehicles are among a col-lection of high-powered trucks, tractors, and other vehicles that don't care much about terrain. The museum is open Saturdays and Sundays through-out the summer. Clintonville is located at the junction of U.S. Highway 45 and Wisconsin Highway 22 in Waupaca County.

Although vacations are a time for rock collecting, just don't try to walk off with a section of the Great Wall of China, which is among the stones gathered from around the world and exhibited in **Pioneer Park.** Rocks from Jerusalem, Yellowstone National Park, the Dakota Badlands, and the Arizona Petrified Forest are among the pieces. For specifics on the collection and the Four-Wheel Drive Museum, talk with the folks at the Clintonville Area Chamber of Commerce, 8 North Main Street (715–823–4606). Pioneer Park is located on East 11th Street. The park is open 1:00 to 4:00 P.M. on Sundays and holidays during the summer. A small admission is charged.

DE PERE

The **Oneida Nation Museum** (414–869–2768), 866 Brown County Highway EE, is the repository of materials donated by the "People of the Standing Stone," who came to Wisconsin in the 1880s. The museum, which is open year-round, includes a reproduction of a wood-and-bark longhouse where tribal members used to live. Guides and interpreters are on staff to point visitors in the right direction and talk about the tribe's proud heritage. Admission is $1.00.

De Pere is a suburb of Green Bay and is home to **St. Norbert College.** On the grounds of the ivy-shaded campus is **White Pillars** (414–336–3877), built in 1836 as the first bank building in the state. It now houses the De Pere Historical Society Museum. The building is locat-ed at 403 North Broadway and is open 1:00 to 5:00 P.M., Wednesday through Sunday.

DUNDEE

The **Henry W. Reuss Ice Age Interpretive Center** (414–533–8322) in

Dundee is the hub for information about glaciers that once held Wisconsin in their frosty grip. Part of the 1,000-mile-long **Ice Age Trail,** the center has exhibits on how the rugged contemporary landscape was formed. The facility is located 5 miles east of U.S. Highway 45 on State Highway 67. Have the kids look out the huge picture windows at the center building and identify a moraine, a ridge of rubble that marked the end point of a glacier, or another geographic feature that is now topped by maples and pines. It might be difficult to get them to stretch leg muscles, but get the gang out on the trail to spot black-eyed Susans, feel the wind in their hair, and experience firsthand the living land. Reuss was a Wisconsin congressman who advocated the establishment of the trail and has subsequently worked tirelessly to see that it comes to completion.

The visitor center is open all year, weekdays 8:30 A.M. to 4:00 P.M. and Saturdays and Sundays 9:30 A.M. to 5:00 P.M. A state park sticker is required. A resident daily pass is $4.00, with a nonresident daily pass at $6.00. Resident annual passes are $15 and nonresident annual passes are $24. Before parking, motor vehicles must have an admission ticket attached to the inside of the windshield on the driver's side.

EAGLE RIVER

Loud, racy, explosive . . . and cold. That's the **World Championship Snowmobile Derby** in Eagle River, held on an oval of ice where speeds exceeding than 100 miles per hour can be reached. Tell the kids to wear their long johns and extra wool socks because the windchill at the town track can go down, down, down into the double digits on the minus side. Don't forget the mufflers, both for the warmth and to soften the sound of hundreds of snowmobiles revving at top speed. Yet sled drivers from around the world don't seem to mind the nip in the air. In fact, the frostier the better because all that snow and ice provides plenty of danger and real-life adventure. The behind-the-scenes work is just as fascinating, from the busy pit crews to the water truck struggling around the track to spray another coat of glaze over the glare. The vehicle looks like Old Man Winter incarnate, with its frozen hoses and icicles hanging from every knob and pipe. Don't worry about frostbite, however. Plenty of concession stands are on hand to keep funneling explosive chili and marshmallowy hot choco-late down the throats of the young'uns. For dates, times, and ticket infor-mation, contact the derby at 111 West Pine Street, Box 1447, Eagle River 54521 (715–479–4424 or 479–2764).

The **Snowmobile Racing Hall of Fame,** at the same offices as the derby headquarters, is open 8:30 A.M. to 4:30 P.M. Monday through Friday. Derby artifacts, oodles of photos, and racing machines themselves are dis-played there. The kids can then dream about their future on the track someday.

Until then try the family hand at a cross-country snowmobile adven-ture with **Decker's Sno-Venture Tours** (715–479–2764). The company has led caravans of sledders over hill and vale in Yellowstone National Park and Iceland, as well around the upper Midwest. Thousands of miles of groomed track loop around Eagle River, home base for the tour firm. Decker's takes visitors of all ages on runs up to the Lake Superior shoreline, across the forestland to neighboring counties, and generally wherever there is a trail link. Some trips last up to a week, so be sure there are clean woolies for the youngsters on the ride. Safety first is always the Decker motto, with each rider in line responsible for the driver on both front and back. No one is ever left behind to confront the frozen vastlands alone. Tyro sledders, including kids, can enjoy the trips.

The snowmobile tours over a variety of routes depart from Eagle River Snowmobile Racetrack, on U.S. Highway 45 North in Eagle River. They leave Sundays at 10:00 A.M. and weekdays at 8:30 A.M., returning Fridays during the winter season (depending on snow conditions, so call in advance to confirm). Tours arrive at their overnight lodgings along their respective trails by 4:00 P.M., with runs totaling about 100 miles per day. Costs vary according to what tours are taken, but a week-long expedition from Eagle River to Copper Harbor, Michigan, costs $585 for six days and five nights for the 660-mile round-trip jaunt. That particular tour includes a stop in picturesque Bayfield, Wisconsin, on the frozen Lake Superior shoreline.

Decker's rates include lodgings, meals, guides, and use of the follow-up repair trucks if necessary. Participants can bring their own snowmobiles or rent them from local dealers throughout the area at about $100 per day.

Rentals are also available from the tour company at $300 apiece. Everyone is responsible for buying their own gas. Rental of clothing ranges from $10 to $20 per day, depending on what suits, boots, gloves, hats, or other needs are required.

If kids can pilot a snowmobile, they pay full rate on the tour. Remember that in Wisconsin, as with most other Midwestern states, drivers from twelve to sixteen need to have a snowmobile permit; all others need a valid driver's license. To get a free permit, the child needs to take a written and driving exam at a state Department of Transportation driver's license station or at a Department of Natural Resources office.

Carl's Wood Museum, 1230 Sundstein Road, in Eagle River (715–479–8379), is a place to go if the jokester in the backseat of the family caravan wants to "knock on wood" or if Dad needs to see a real chip off the old block. For a rip-roaring sight, take a gander at Carl's carvings whacked from huge logs by means of chainsaws. There's even a 2,000-pound, fierce-looking grizzly sculpture that looks hungry enough to eat . . . termites.

Admission is $4.00 for adults. Seniors are $3.00, with kids ages sixteen and under $2.00. The museum is open 9:00 A.M. to 5:00 P.M. Mondays through Saturdays and 10:00 A.M. to 4:00 P.M. Sundays from late May through Labor Day. It is also open 10:00 A.M. to 5:00 P.M. daily from Labor Day through early October. The outgoing, loquacious Carl of the shop, Carl Schels, was born in Bavaria in 1907. He is still active with his craft, which he learned as a trapper in Minnesota's far northern wilderness. Schels even wrote a book about his experiences called *Trapper's Legacy.*

ELKHART LAKE

Follow County Highway A from Greenbush to Glenbeulah to Elkhart Lake, in the heart of Kettle Moraine Country. The rolling hills and ridges were formed by glaciers 10,000 years ago, making the **Road America course** at Elkhart Lake a racer's twisting, turning nightmare. Which is why fans and drivers love the 4-mile-long fabled track, tucked into the woods just off State Highway 67. Film star and race hound Paul Newman often shows up here to demonstrate that he still has the right stuff. In fact, portions of his movie *Winning* were filmed here. The race season extends through summer and into autumn, with a full complement of events for formula cars and high-powered machinery of other styles. Any event here is a social extravaganza, with champagne and canapés on the grassy hummocks, where most folks sit to watch the action. Kids, of course, are welcome. Tickets range from $10 to $20. For dates contact Road America at (414) 892–4576 or (800) 365–RACE.

EPHRAIM

Located on the windy Green Bay side of Door County, this tiny fishing village has long been a favorite of water sports fans. Sailors and sailboarders appreciate the fresh breezes that rip around the point from the north on their blustery way southward. Rentals of sailboarding equipment are available at **Windsurf Door County,** 9876 Water Street (414–854–4071), with oodles of sailing stuff available at **Ephraim Sailing Center** on South Shore Pier (414–854–4336).

Ephraim is also the entry point to **Peninsula State Park** (414–868–3258), one of Wisconsin's most popular parks due to its location on a bluff towering over the dark rugged waters of Green Bay. Camping is possible, both in the crowning woods and near the beach. Since the park is open year-round, it is a constant haven for cyclists, hikers, snowshoers, skiers, and snowmobilers during their respective seasons. The park also has the only state-owned golf course, an eighteen-holer where Ma can catch up on her hole-in-one form while Pop takes the gang to the lighthouse at Eagle Bluff for a look over the water. Peninsula State Park is tucked between Fish Creek and Ephraim on Wisconsin Highway 42. The park, one of the most popular in the state, is well marked from the highway.

One of the best places in the tiny community for sailing instructions is **Ephraim Sailing and Windsurfing Center** (414–854–4324) on South Shore Pier. Call for summer lesson rates and class hours. But if a guest prefers scooting along the waves with someone else at the tiller, call **Bella Sailing Cruises** (414–854–BOAT) for a $25 two-hour nautical jaunt from South Shore Pier, around Horseshoe Island, and past the caves on Eagle Bluff.

FOND DU LAC

The tykes will be amazed at Fond du Lac's **Talking Houses.** The city has prepared a neat tour around town whereby the car radio can pick up a special program that describes eleven of twenty-three historic sites. The Fond du Lac Information Center, 19 Scott Street (414–923–3010 or 800–937–9123), has maps and details on how the system works. Driving slowly past the Victorian-era homes is a fun excursion, especially while on the way to **Lakeside Park** on the shore of the 137,000-acre Lake Winnebago, where Main Street dead-ends on the north side of town.

From mid-April to mid-October, the old lighthouse in the park is open daily 8:00 A.M. to dusk so guests can clamber to the observation deck. From Memorial Day through Labor Day, the petting zoo is open 1:00 to 3:00 P.M. weekdays and 11:00 A.M. to 3:00 P.M. on weekends and holidays. The miniature train, roto-whip, carousel, bumper boats, aqua bikes, and canoe rental are open 11:00 A.M. to 8:30 P.M. Monday through Saturday and 10:00 A.M. to 8:30 P.M. Sunday. The rides are free. For information on the park, call the Fond du Lac information center at the number given above.

GREEN BAY

The city of Green Bay proudly calls itself the Birthplace of the Midwest, dating its westernized history from 1634, when explorer Jean Nicolet beached his canoe and said "Howdy" (actually, *"Bon jour"*) to the Winnebago who had already been living there for generations. According to legend, apparently the Frenchman thought he was at some outpost of the Chinese Empire because he leaped from his canoe wearing a hand-made silk damask robe with colorful handstitched birds and flowers. He then proceeded to fire two pistols into the area to announce his arrival. This was probably a rather puzzling custom in the eyes of the locals, but they invited him to dinner of beaver tails and wild rice anyway, the first of several feasts that attracted thousands of curious Native Americans from throughout the area. Nicolet then paddled off to claim more territory for France, supposedly taking his sartorial splendor with him.

Today Green Bay is more noted for being the Toilet Paper Capital of the World. This is a dubious distinction for one of Wisconsin's most major and oldest cities, but one that youngsters—with their affinity for discussing bodily functions at the most inappropriate times—would certainly find amusing. Actually, the title is well earned, but add on other paper products as well. Wood-processing plants, mills, and paper company offices form the core of the city's business world. The folks here, however, don't just eat, drink, and chew on newly made toothpicks. For many the **Green Bay Packers** football team is IT. World champions—at various times—the Packers are community owned . . . monetarily, emotionally, and spiritually. The Packers are the country's oldest professional football team, organized in 1919 and receiving a pro franchise in 1921. They were the first to win three NFL championships in a row, the first Super Bowl champs, and the first team to have its own hall of fame. The team received its name because its first corporate sponsor was the Acme Packing Company, a major Green Bay employer at the time.

Few kids in Wisconsin, except for some on the western fringes of the St. Croix River Valley that abuts Minnesota (these might be stray Vikings fans) or one or two along the border with Illinois (having a predilection for the Chicago Bears), would ever dream of not wearing the state team's green and gold. The Pack's **Hall of Fame** has a hushed, meccalike quality about its polished halls and glassed displays of shoulder pads, trophies, shoes, and autographed pigskins. Row after row of football greats, from renowned players like Bart Starr to fabled coaches like Vince Lombardi, peer down from their portrait frames. Their eyes follow visitors everywhere.

The Hall of Fame is open 10:00 A.M. to 5:00 P.M. daily (except Christmas Day) at 855 Lombardi Avenue (U.S. Highway 41), directly across the street from Lambeau Field, where the team's gladiators have battled their enemies for more than a half-century. Admission to the Hall of Fame is $6.00 for adults, $3.50 for youngsters six to fifteen. Seniors and family rates are also available. The backseat squad can help dads (or moms) keep their driving eyes peeled for the giant player leaping atop a football, the sculpture that indicates the museum's entrance. Tours can also be arranged to see the field and survey all the behind-the-scenes action, from the press box to the sky boxes. Call (800) 499–4281 for details.

Train robbers find willing "victims aboard the rolling stock of the National Railroad Museum. (Courtesy Green Bay Area Visitor and Convention Bureau)

Railroad fans in the family will love all the steel and muscle evidenced by the old-time locomotives at the **National Railroad Museum,** 2285 South Broadway (414–435–7245). More than eighty pieces of rolling stock, from monster engines to oil tankers to a refrigerator car and tail-ending cabooses, are displayed on tracks ringing the facility's grounds. Puffing, huffing steamers and sleek diesels show the technical progression in these fabulous annals of transportation history. Included is General Dwight D. Eisenhower's World War II traveling staff car, which operated under the code name Bayonet. Take the littlest kid in the family and place him or her alongside the Union Pacific Big Boy for a photograph. Shutterbugs will need wide-angle lenses because the 1941 engine is the largest locomotive ever built. It weighs more than 600 tons and is 133 feet long, half the length of a football field. Everyone should trek through the displays in the main museum building and watch the slide/video presentation there, to pick up a sense of background. Then run to the outside, where hands-on, all-aboard climbing is allowed on some of the larger locomotives. Just watch your head. For any youngster needing to conduct research for a school paper, the museum has an excellent library of railroad materials. Since the heart of nineteenth-century America was the railroad depot, it is appropriate that the hub of activity at the train museum is also a depot. Thousands of pieces of memorabilia are displayed in the Hood Junction Depot, a reproduction of such a structure in Langley, South Carolina. The museum is open 9:00 A.M. to 5:00 P.M. daily. Admission rates are $16.00 for a family of four in summer; $8.00 in winter. Individual prices are also available.

Moving from indoors to outside, the **Bay Beach Wildlife Sanctuary** (414–391–3671) on Green Bay's far north side Sanctuary Road is the place to put nature into perspective. Some 700 acres of nature trails and cross-country ski trails are available for silent pursuits. To get to Bay Beach from I–43, take the Webster Avenue exit (187) and go east. Just look for the signage. A wildlife observation platform allows the littlest child to see above the brush and trees, in the hope of spotting a deer. The sanctuary is free, but donations are accepted. The trails and nature center building are open daily year-round.

Once the gang gets tired of counting hawks, swallows, woodpeckers, rabbits, chipmunks, and other feathered or furry denizens of the wilds, take everyone down the road to the **Bay Beach Amusement Park,** 1313 Beach Drive (414–448–3365). The free park has softball fields, horseshoe pits, volleyball courts, kiddie rides (most still cost only 10 cents). The park is open 10:00 A.M. to 6:00 P.M., Saturdays and Sundays, mid-April through Memorial Day; 10:00 A.M. to 9:00 P.M. daily through Labor Day; and 10:00 A.M. to 6:00 P.M. daily through September.

GREENBUSH

The Wisconsin State Historical Society operates the **Wade House Stagecoach Inn & Wisconsin Carriage Museum** (414–526–3271), which takes guests into the past century. Built in 1850, the refurbished Wade House, an old stagecoach inn at W7747 Plank Road in the old cross-roads village, has three floors now open to the public. The adjacent carriage museum has a hundred horse-drawn carts, wagons, sleds, and farm implements dating back generations. A dirt road links the carriage museum to the Wade House, with visitors being transported in a horse-drawn shuttle to keep the proper mood. The outbuildings include a blacksmith shop and a smokehouse. Each September Civil War reenactors fill the grounds and turn the entire site into a real-life camp. On a field behind the buildings, Union and Confederate forces stage mock battles, complete with cavalry charges, blasting cannon, and bayonet charges. The fighting takes place along an original sunken road and stone wall, reminiscent of many actual battles in the horrific War Between the States. Crowds six to ten deep line the periphery of the action, sometimes making it hard for smaller kids to see. But wiggly ones can squirm through legs to the front of the audience for a better look. Military encampments, with sutlers offering clothing, muskets, and other nineteenth-century items for sale, are nearby, where youngsters can talk with the reenactors about their uniforms and lifestyles.

The complex is easy to find, being located 20 miles west of Sheboygan or 20 miles east of Fond du Lac on Wisconsin Highway 23. The house and grounds are open 9:00 A.M. to 5:00 P.M. daily from May 1 through October 31, with admission at $5.00 adults and $2.00 for children five to twelve.

GREEN LAKE

The 1,001-acre **American Baptist Green Lake Center,** on Wisconsin Highway 23, about 4 miles west of the city of Green Lake, (414–294–3323) has extensive camping, swimming, and golfing options and is open to the public. While in the area, take a cruise on the *Yachts of Fun.* The excursion vessel is boarded from the Heidel House Resort docks (414–294–3344 or 800–444–2812). Daily cruises are offered June through August and on Saturdays and Sundays in May, September, and October. Call for the boat schedules and prices.

HORICON

The best bullhead fishing in the state can be had at the **Horicon Marsh,** with grassy banks in town leading to the water's edge, making it a great spot for tiny first-time fisherfolk. Canoeing is another good way to get far back into the reeds and brush to birdwatch, angle for bass, and generally get away from the rush of daily life. The marsh is generally bounded on the south by Wisconsin Highway 33, on the west by Wisconsin Highway 26, the north by Wisconsin Highway 49, and the east by Dodge County Highway V. The 34-mile Wild Goose Trail skirts the western edge of the marsh and is available for hikers and bikers, as well as cross-country skiers and snowmobilers in the winter.

Blue Heron Tours (414–485–2942) takes regular hour-plus runs into the marsh aboard houseboats, offering an up-close view of the watery haven for all sorts of wildlife. The area is administered by the Wisconsin Department of Natural Resources from its office at 1210 Palmatory Road (414–485–3000). Drop by or call to ask questions. The marsh is a National Wildlife Refuge, so the feds are also involved. Their offices (414–387–2658) are at W4279 Headquarters Road in nearby Mayville.

It is autumn when the marsh comes most alive. Tens of thousands of Canada geese pause there each season on their way to goose condos farther south, far away from the upper Midwest's winter chill. The 31,000-acre site is a veritable vacation resort for the feathered flocks as they zoom in overhead, honking and beeping in their V-formations. Local farmers groan when the birds arrive because they often take snack time in nearby cornfields. Yet watching the flocks is easy. Any road around the marsh is a prime viewing area. In fact, after a while the sheer number of birds can be overwhelming. Be sure to watch where people step if they want to get out of the car for a closer look. Goose droppings are large and stinky, not the thing to be smushed underfoot and carried back into the close confines of an auto.

IOLA

The annual **Iola Old Car Show and Swap Meet,** held in early July, is considered one of the largest such antique auto shows in the world. Up to 2,500 old-time flivvers flock to the event, which attracts 100,000 people. Collectors in the family can pick up hubcaps, crank handles, rumble seats, hood ornaments, steering wheels, transmissions, and, of course, entire cars. So no one becomes lost, be sure to choose an assembly point at a definite reunion time for kids, who naturally want to scoot around the grounds on their own to check out tailpipes and ignition systems.

The grounds are located less than a mile east of Wisconsin Highway 49, less than 1 block south of Wisconsin Highway 161. Look for signage at least 5 miles down Highway 49. For information on the show and each year's dates, call (715) 445–4000. Admission is $4.00 per day or $8.00 for a weekend pass. Ages twelve and under are $2.00 per day or $4.00 for weekend pass; youngsters five and under are free. Hours are 6:00 A.M. to 9:00 P.M. Saturday and 6:00 A.M. to 5:00 P.M. Sunday. These car lovers are obviously early risers.

KOHLER

Home of the famous Kohler Company, whose bathroom fixtures grace castles, airports, and residences around the world, Kohler was originally a planned village for the company's workers. Today the main building, which once housed immigrant employees, is the **American Club** (414–457–8000), the only five-diamond resort property in Wisconsin. Black Wolf Run, one of the toughest golf courses in the country, is adjacent to the American Club. Most fun is to stroll through the **Kohler Design Center** (414–457–3699), which showcases all the firm's latest bathroom technicalities, from bathtubs with sidedoors to climate-controlled booths for a "sense-around" sensation. Noted interior designers vie for the opportunity to feature their work in a series of model rooms around the center, to demonstrate how fancy one's shower room can really be. Kids will get a kick out of the Great Wall of China, an intricate two-story-tall pattern made by multicolored toilet bowls. The design center, which is located on Highland Drive in Kohler, is open daily at no charge.

A short walk to the north of the design center is a mall featuring other decoration and construction elements for the home, from mosaics to woodworking. Individual shops cater to highly refined tastes and to folks who appreciate quality. The Kohler Company also sponsors artists in a grant program whereby they develop their skills in various media while working alongside regular laborers. The resulting sculptures dot the Kohler

Company factory and grounds. Even mistakes can be turned into a suc-cesful challenge at the plant. One artist made a cast-iron deer, but the sculpture's back collapsed in the foundry during its final preparation. Rather than dump the piece, the artist cut off the offending iron and made the rest of the deer into a life-size charcoal grill. Have the kids try to spot the grizzly bear, rearing up on its hind legs.

The firm sponsors a real down-home Fourth of July, with band con-certs so rousing that they would make march composer John Philip Sousa want to rise up again with his baton at the ready. Of course, there are fire-works, plenty of bunting and fluttering flags, and kids' activities to round out the holiday. At Christmas a chocolate-tasting party is hosted at the American Club, presenting enough caloric delights to turn the head of any-one within 20 miles who has a sweet tooth. This latter event is not kid-oriented, but it gives Mom and Dad a swishy night out on the town, with glowing candles, glittering silver, romantic music, and, why not?—maybe even an overnight getaway in a large gracious room, with bath facilities rivaling those in a Kuwati palace.

LAONA

The **Lumberjack Special & Camp Five Museum & Ecology Complex** (715–674–3414) is only ⅓ mile west of the junction of Highways 8 and 32. But the museum is more than a simple highway crossing. It is a trip into the past, where kids can ogle huge stacks of cut timber and touch rough lumber. For decades, as the nineteenth century moved into the twentieth, the vast white pine forests of northern Wisconsin gave up their treasures to the logging crews. Tens of thousands of board feet of wood fed the appetite of a growing America. No wonder Forest County got its name. The Lumberjack Special, a 1916-era steam train, takes visitors from the Laona Depot through the woods to the Camp Five Museum Complex, where the tough life of the logging camp is highlighted. The museum fea-tures audiovisual exhibits, a working blacksmith shop complete with brawny smith and roaring forge, a harness-making shop, and a country store. Surrey rides through the woods are also available, as are pontoon excursions on the nearby Red River. The train runs from mid-June to the last Saturday in August, with rides on the hour between 10:00 A.M. and 2:00 P.M., Monday through Saturday. Fall color trips can be taken on Saturdays and Sundays from September through early October. There is a small fee for the rides.

MANAWA

Although the city was founded by lumbermen and evolved into an agricul-tural center, the folks who live in Manawa are enamored of all things hav-ing to do with the Wild West. The July 4th weekend in Manawa hosts the annual **Midwestern Rodeo,** which went into its thirty-seventh year in 1995. Sanctioned by the Professional Rodeo Cowboys Association, the three-day hee-haw includes bareback bronco and saddle bronco riding, calf roping, steer wrestling, bull riding, team roping, and girls' barrel racing. Competitors come from around the country and Canada, eyeing the almost $10,000 in cash prizes for the cowpokes who can make the time limit.

The rodeo is sponsored by the Manawa Lions Club. Visitors cheer for their favorite cowgirls in the Miss Rodeo Wisconsin Pageant and take in the parade that kicks off the festivities. There are also free dances (for all ages) on the Friday and Saturday nights of the rodeo weekend, a chicken barbecue on the grounds, prize drawings, and pony rides. The rodeo grounds are located on a sixteen-and-a-half-acre site in southwest Manawa.

Rodeo events are held at 7:00 P.M. on Friday, at 2:00 and 8:00 P.M. Saturday, and 2:00 P.M. Sunday. Tickets for $7.50 reserved seats must be purchased in advance by contacting Midwestern Rodeo, Box 244, Manawa 54949 (414–596–2005). General admission is $6.50 for adults and $2.00 for kids twelve and under.

MANITOWOC

A submarine in Wisconsin? Sure enough, the USS *Cobia* is berthed in downtown Manitowoc, as an attraction to be toured at the **Manitowoc Maritime Museum,** at 75 Maritime Drive (414–684–0218). The deadly vessel saw heavy action in World War II and was moved to the city after-ward to augment the museum's burgeoning collection of seagoing artifacts.

The *Cobia* is now considered a National Historic Landmark, typical of the many submarines built in the city's shipyards during the war. Visitors can crawl along the narrow passageways, look into wardrooms, scramble up ladders to hatches that open to a glimpse of the sun, and generally marvel that fighting men actually lived aboard the craft for months at a time. The museum, with its 21,000 square feet of exhibit space, is the largest such facility on the Great Lakes and even includes an entire nineteenth-century waterfront scene inside its main building. It is open daily year-round from 9:00 A.M. to 5:00 P.M.

The **Chippewa** excursion boat (414–682–8111) provides a narrated cruise down the river, past the Cobia and on to the once bustling shipyards. Board near the submarine landing, where there is plenty of parking. The tours, at a small fee, are conducted May through mid-October.

While strolling the streets of this historic lake town, take the gang into **Beerntsen's Candies,** 108 North Eighth Street (414–684–9616), for some eye-filling wonders. Homemade chocolates and other temptations fill shelf after shelf in this tiny store, which has the ambience of an old-time soda shop. Beernsten's has been a traditional gathering place in Manitowoc for several generations, but there has never been a Weight Watchers meeting held at the shop, at least not to anyone's recent knowledge. And dentists smile as they pass by, looking in the great front windows at the kids munching away inside. But who cares? Sit in one of the old booths and order something totally sinful in the dietary sense. There are plenty of napkins to wipe messy little faces and sticky hands, so do it!

Since food somehow seems to be on everyone's mind all of a sudden, swing the family over to the **Pine River Dairy** (414–758–2233) at 10115 English Avenue to watch butter being made. Come early in the morning, although the plant is open until 4:00 P.M. Then there are the bakeries of the **Natural Ovens of Manitowoc,** which features lusciously crusty bread and rolls (these go great with Pine River butter). No one will find mushy fake bread here, only heavy stuff with whole grains and a great crunchy texture that tastes and sounds like real bread should. Natural Ovens Bakery (414–758–2500) is located at 4300 County Highway CR at the edge of the city. Follow the nose.

Since all the folks have to now work off the poundage gained from chocolate, dairy products, and dough, tour **Zunker's Antique Car Museum,** 3722 MacArthur Drive, to marvel at how autos caught on in the public's imagination. A few of the early cars seem as if they couldn't make it up a small bump with a strong tailwind. Some eighty years of transportation history unfold at the museum, whose lively exhibits and knowledgeable staff keep young people alert and not thinking about simply getting to their sixteenth birthdays and snaring a license to drive. Zunker's is open daily May through mid-September. Admission is charged.

MOUNTAIN

"For the want of a shoe . . ." the old ditty goes. In horseshoe pitching, a strong arm is needed. Especially during the first full weekend in August, when this tiny town hosts the **Mountain Open Pitching Tournament.** Rounds begin at 8:00 A.M. and end whenever the last clink is heard on Sunday. Several hundred pitchers gather from around the state, making it the largest such event in the region. There are several classes, accommodating teens to old-timers. Trophies and cash prizes are awarded to the winners. A baseball tournament and a flea market complete the activities. The tournament site is located 1½ miles south of Mountain on Highways 32 and 64, adjacent to the village community center. Call (715) 276–7345 or 276–6103 for registration and other details.

NEW LONDON

"A-tubing we will go, a-tubing we will go. Hi, ho, the derry-o, a-tubing we will go." OK, so the song isn't much, but the fun is there. The smooth flowage of the Wolf River is great for a leisurely float trip on a hot summer afternoon (just bring sunscreen lotion because the sun reflecting off the water can make for fiery pink skin). One of Wisconsin's finest river beaches for tube launching, canoeing, and swimming is found at **Wolf River Trips and Campground** (414–982–2458) on Route 3, 2 miles west of New London. Take County Road X west from New London or Highway X east from Weyauwega. Either way, travelers are not far off Highways 54, 110, 45, or 22.

There is a definite tubing technique that sets the pros apart from the tyros. To make it into the upper echelons from the lower ranks, take this advice: Toss the tube into the water, yell, jump into the tube, bob around to get used to the cool water, then start drifting downstream. Sounds easy enough, right? Because it's the yelling and amount of bobbing that make the difference. Wolf River makes sure moms and dads won't have to worry about kids, since life preservers are provided for the smaller floaters. A free shuttle picks up drifters several miles downriver. Floaters can take as many trips as they can cram in between 9:00 A.M. and 5:00 P.M. daily during the summer. Rental rates are generally higher on Friday, Saturday, and Sunday ($4.50 plus $1.00 deposit) than on weekdays ($3.50 plus $1.00 deposit).

The property also has canoes for more of a frontier experience. Excursions run 9:00 A.M. to 4:00 P.M. daily, including two-hour, four-hour, and one-day expeditions, wiggling their way south from the campgrounds. The Wolf is as curvy as country-western Dolly Parton, so some amount of steering and paddling is necessary. But beginners can have just as much fun as old-timers. Float fishing is allowed.

After all that whooping it up on the river, suntanned (or burned) families appreciate easing into the cool, dim interiors of the Pine Tree, the Rainbow, or any other of the supper clubs throughout the New London vicinity. Afterward campers at Wolf River can take in shuffleboard, horseshoes, tennis, swimming in the river, volleyball, and softball. It's enough to have vacationers return home for a rest.

OSHKOSH

Yes, Oshkosh is the home of the big B'Gosh, the casual clothing manufacturer whose brand name is famous around the world. Parents with an eye on the budget can stop at the 230,000-square-foot **Manufacturers Marketplace,** with its Oshkosh B'Gosh factory outlet called the **Genuine Article** (414–426–5817). Clothes there range from the traditional striped coveralls to toddlers' wear. Another sixty stores in the mall, 3001 South Washburn Street (800–866–5900), provide teenagers with innumerable choices in which to roam.

Across the highway is the **EAA Air Adventure Museum** (414–

426–4818), showing the progress made in air transportation over the years. The museum is located at 3000 Poberezny Road, easily accessible off U.S. Highway 41. For a landmark, look for the Sabre jet on its pedestal near the exit from the highway. Each summer the EAA stages the largest "fly-in" in the world, with hundreds of planes coming and going like so many gnats. The planes range from the supersonic Concorde to home-made, lighter-than-air devices that look as though they can't get off the ground. In 1994, celebrating the twenty-fifth anniversary of the U.S. space program, several dozen astronauts, including the original contingent of spacemen, were on hand to meet the crowds. Workshops and lectures round out the program for the thousands of guests who admire the civilian and military aircraft that come from around the world.

The museum is open year-round 8:30 A.M. to 5:00 P.M. Monday through Saturday and 11:00 A.M. to 5:00 P.M. Sunday. Admission is $7.50 for adults, $6.00 for seniors, and $5.50 for kids eight to eighteen. Youngsters seven and under are free.

RHINELANDER

Tell the kids to watch out for **hodags** when driving along dark forest roads in Oneida County around Rhinelander. The fearsome, long-toothed beasts were known for stomping around in the woods, tickling loggers, and generally raising havoc with the rabbit population. But don't push the point too much, terrifying the tykes. The hodag is actually a mythological critter, dreamed up at the turn of the century by some young pranksters who wanted to pull the wool over the eyes of gullible visitors. Still, the hodag has taken on dimensions these jokesters probably never dreamed of, from being the name of the high school mascot to becoming statues on the roofs of restaurants.

On a more realistic level, the city's woodsy history is exemplified at the **Rhinelander Logging Museum** (715–369–5004) in Pioneer Park. This reproduction of a nineteenth-century logging camp is complete with appropriately costumed interpreters. They tell about the rugged life in the forests, showing off original equipment and describing all the personalities who opened up the North Woods to development. Also on the grounds are an 1879 narrow-gauge railroad engine, a rural school, and a Civilian Conservation Corps museum, as well as a Soo Line depot. The museum is open daily 10:30 A.M. to 5:00 P.M. from mid-May through mid-September. Donations are requested.

RIPON

Personal voting preference and politics aside, take the kids to see the **Little White Schoolhouse** (414–748–6764) on Blackburn Street, just down the hill from Ripon College. The building is considered the birthplace of the Republican party, which was organized in 1854. Some upstart communities outside Wisconsin, however, have claimed the same honor. Naturally, Riponites pooh-pooh them as specious latecomers. The little building is open for tours Monday through Saturday 10:00 A.M. to 4:00 P.M. and Sunday noon to 4:00 P.M. Memorial Day through Labor Day. It is open only on Saturday and Sunday in early May, September, and October. At other times visitors can peek in the windows and see lots of pictures of bewhiskered old gents on the walls, plus party artifacts in glass display cases. The windows are low enough so Junior and Missy can even sneak a gander at this GOP gestation site.

Larson's Famous Clydesdales (414–748–5466) on Route 1 in Reed's Corner, near Ripon, offers a chance to meet animals up close, and here Clydesdale colts can be petted. Covered bleacher seats allow guests to watch a harness show in relative comfort, even on the hottest summer days. The huge horses are surprisingly lighted-footed as they go through their intricate paces. The Larson family also has a large collection of antique wagons and similar horse-drawn equipment. Larson's is open daily in the summer months, with numerous motorcoach tours taking advantage of the program. Admission is charged.

SEYMOUR

Snug in a harness suspended from an overhead crane, the chef at Seymour's **Hamburger Celebration** swings back and forth across hundreds of sizzling patties. Sprinkling careful doses of salt and pepper, he sweeps over the giant fry pan. "It's a hot job but it's gotta be done, well done," he says, wiping the sweat from his brow after the Peter Pan routine. This routine, accompanied by laughs and plenty of applause from onlookers, is part of the fun at the festival. The feast-fest is held the first Saturday in August, celebrating the birth of the burger. According to town legend, a local meatball salesman named Charlie Nagreen fried up a batch of patty-shaped ground meat at the Outagamie Fair in 1855. By squishing meatballs and slapping them between buns, the momentous occasion supposedly introduced the first real hamburger to a hungry pre-McDonald's public.

The celebration is held at the Outagamie County Fairgrounds, starting at 8:00 A.M. A parade, led by Hamburger Patty and Bunard, meanders down Main Street at midday. A Hamburger Olympics, open to all comers, concludes the afternoon with such events as a ketchup slide. Call 414–833–6800.

The fairgrounds are located on the north side of the city. Simply take Wisconsin Highway 55N/Outagamie County Highway C (Main Street), or follow the wonderful perfume of frying burgers. Tickets are $2.00 in advance and $3.00 at the gate.

SHAWANO

Heritage Park, tucked into a bend of the roaring Wolf River at the dead end of Franklin Street in Shawano, is a cluster of restored historical structures that includes a country schoolhouse (stick the kids in their desks and help 'em recite the day's poetry lesson), barns and outbuildings, and a log cabin. Costumed interpreters help with all the background from June through September. Call (715) 526–3323 or (800) 235–8528. A donation is suggested. Sunset Island next door has picnic shelters, a fishing dock, and a boat launch.

SHEBOYGAN

Here's a hint for getting along well in Sheboygan: Never, never ask for a weiner when you really mean a brat (and that is not the grumpy thirteen-year-old who just pounded her younger sister in the back of the van). The term is *braaaaat,* with a short *a.* The difference between the two is like seeking a gourmet meal as compared with a bowl of dry cornflakes. Sheboygan is also home to **Bratwurst Day,** held on the first Saturday in August. This is a real family festival, during which the city's tree-shaded Fountain Park downtown hosts folksingers, hands-on crafts for kids, and tons and tons of brats cooked over open fires. The picnic feast is not complete without roasted corn on the cob and vanilla ice cream sundaes lathered with strawberries. Let Junior try a brat pizza; Mom can handle a brat taco, while Dad and Sis can stick to traditional brats hidden in their monster buns, dolloped with nose-tickling German mustard and layered with onions and/or sauerkraut. The event is free, except for foods and beverages.

Out at Kiwanis Park on the northwest side of town, nationally known musical entertainers and acrobats, elephant trainers, and clowns from Walker Brothers Circus put on free shows. Polka bands do their foot-stomping, twirl-around routine as well. True to the family nature of things, no beer is served downtown, but it is available at the outlying park.

A parade along Main Street kicks off Brat Day, where it seems everyone in town marches along happily waving to friends, including the county coroner, politicians of every stripe and party, kids on unicycles, grandmas on Rollerblades, and donors to the Red Cross blood bank. Perch anywhere along the downtown route for the procession, which sometimes has run up to two hours (little kids watching might become antsy). But that's no time problem for most of the locals, because they know that plenty of brats await them at either park. "We've never run out of brats," assert well-fed organizers from the sponsoring Jaycees. And even if there was ever a hint of such a calamity, the city is the home headquarters of the Johnsonville Foods Company (JFC), which makes links by the megaton every day. JFC could fill any potential void in seconds. For dates and details about Brat Day, contact the Sheboygan Area Convention & Visitors Bureau (CVB), 631 New York Avenue, Sheboygan 53081 (414–457–9495).

There is hardly anything better on a broiling summer day than to swoosh down the Aqua Avalanche waterslide at **Jaycee Park** on Sheboygan's north side off Business Highway 42. Family fun in the park also includes fishing, boating, and a swimming beach. If the kids have already loaded up on brats, wait an hour to digest the goodies before

Anglers young and old get hooked on charter fishing on the waters of Lake Michigan.
(Courtesy Manitowoc Visitor and Convention Bureau)

attempting an Aqua-experience. Jaycee Park is open noon to 8:00 P.M. daily, Memorial Day to Labor Day. An all-day pass is $3.50; a book of seven-day passes is $19.95. Call the CVB at the number above for details.

Or try a Lake Michigan charter-fishing jaunt in search of the elusive lake trout or giant German brown trout. Half-day rates range from $55 and $65 per person, with a boat rental minimum of $200. Even little kids can have a heyday out on the waves. Everyone aboard gets a turn at hauling in a fish as well. But pack a picnic lunch if a captain doesn't offer such services (be sure to ask when contracting with a vessel) as the rumble from empty young stomachs is disconcerting to fish. If there are enough fisherfolk in one family, rent the whole boat for a morning or an afternoon cruise. Otherwise the captain will fill up a charter with other folks. Sheboygan is a center for the state's charter-fishing fleet, with dozens of qualified guides ready to help bring in the lunkers. To find a crew, obtain a copy of the Wisconsin State Charter Fishing Association membership roster from Doug Carlstrom, 1625 North Fourth Street, Sheboygan 53081 (414–459–7905). There are some 150 members in the organization.

STURGEON BAY

The city is the entryway to Wisconsin's **Door County,** a vacation playground that has lost some of its pristine charm due to developers and their malls and big resorts. But the major part of the peninsula is safe for the moment. Sturgeon Bay is an old waterfront town that has been scrubbed and spruced up for its second hundred years.

Haul the crew off to the **Door County Maritime Museum** (414–743–8139) at the foot of Florida Street. There they can get a sense of regional history, with pictures of steamers and stories of sunken vessels to keep up the interest. The museum is open daily Memorial Day to mid-October, 10:00 A.M. to 4:00 P.M. and until 8:00 P.M. on Fridays and Saturdays. It is also open weekends in early May and late October. There is no admission charge, but donations are requested.

For a landlubber's view of Door County, climb up the observation tower at **Potawatomi State Park** (414–746–2890). When the sky is a rich cobalt and the sun is brightly shining, visitors can spy Marinette, across Green Bay to the west, and Chambers Island, 20 miles to the northeast. On a foggy day anyone would be lucky to spot the hand in front of his or her face. But a trip to the tower is worth it regardless of the weather. The state park entrance is located at 3740 Park Drive.

From Sturgeon Bay head north for biking, cherry picking, perusing art galleries, charter fishing, camping, cross-country skiing, golf, and amusement parks. Door County has at least 250 miles of in-and-out coastline, a figure cartographers say exceeds that of any other single county in the United States. Have the kids write that fact down in their vacation tour report.

While in Door County, sample a traditional **fish boil,** which restaurateurs perform with great gusto and flair. Potatoes, onions, and Lake Michigan whitefish or trout are boiled in a huge kettle over an open flame. As the mixture comes to a magnificent head, kerosene is poured on the flames to produce an explosive boil-over that removes the fat from the liquid in the pot. While the little ones should see how the process is done, be sure they don't get too close to the fire. Singed eyebrows on holiday is no one's idea of fun.

The Door County Chamber of Commerce is the fount of all knowledge when it comes to fish boils, galleries, hiking opportunities, scenic overlooks, park rates, and resort openings. Contact the folks there at Box 406, Sturgeon Bay 54235–0406 (414–743–4456 or 800–52–RELAX).

TWO RIVERS

No, the folks who work at the **Point Beach Energy Center** (414–755–4334) do not glow in the dark. Nor does Bart Simpson's dad work here. But the nuclear power plant, 10 miles north of Two Rivers, is one of the largest along the Great Lakes and provides electricity up and down the western shore of Lake Michigan. Guests are welcome to drop by and tour the facility's exhibition area, which tells of nuclear power's role in energy generation. There are plenty of audiovisual displays, hands-on computer games, and videos to engross the kids, so alert them to that fact while driving up to the front entrance at 6600 Nuclear Road. There is even a nature trail outside the plant that anyone can take for a quick stroll. The energy center is open daily April through October, 8:30 A.M. to 5:00 P.M., and November through March, 10:00 A.M. to 4:30 P.M. Admission is free.

Nearby **Point Beach State Forest** has plenty of camping sites along its beach and in the surrounding forest. To get to both, look for appropriate exit signage along U.S. Highway 43. Call (414) 794–7480.

WAUPACA

J.R.'s Sportsman's Bar and Children's Zoo (715–258–9605; 414–295–3007 in the off-season) in Waupaca is open 9:00 A.M. to 8:00 P.M., seven days a week from Memorial Day through Labor Day, to accommodate crowds of youngsters who love to ogle and pet all sorts of animals, from sheep to zebras. The zoo itself has more than thirty species of critters and birds, while the bar has dozens of mounted animals, including an amazing thirty-two-point buck. Sensitive kids might question the why of that particular display, especially after touring the zoo, with its live residents. So parents should be prepared to answer questions. J.R.'s is located ⅛ mile west of Highway 10 on Highway 54. There is an admission charge to the zoo.

Sparkling Springs Family Adventure Land (715–258–8122) is a water and thrills park, with runs totaling more than 800 feet long and with enough go-carts and mini-carts to stock an Indy 500 race. The passerby can't miss the place, located at the intersection of State Highways 10 and 22 and County Highway K. Manager Jack Mayer keeps the place humming. The facility is open daily 10:00 A.M. until, well, when the crowd thins out in early evening. Rates are $8.53 for unlimited sliding for ages eight and up and less for unlimited sliding for ages five to seven. Kids four and under slide with an adult are are free. Go-carts are $2.99 a ride, but if a guest buys five tickets, they'll get another one free. The mini go-carts are $1.99 per ride. The five-ticket, one bonus also applies here. Group rates are also available.

Tom Thumb Miniature Golf (715–258–8737), N2494 Whispering Pines Road, is about 3 miles west of Waupaca on County Highway Q. The course, which features eighteen interesting hazards themed around fairy tales, is open daily in the summer season 10:00 A.M. to 10:00 P.M. Monday through Saturday and 11:00 A.M. to 10:00 P.M. Sunday. Call for rates.

Ding's Dock (715–258–2612) canoe trips journey down the calm, 3-foot-deep Crystal River, which comes off what is called Wisconsin's Chain of Lakes. From the air the string of beautiful blue water looks like a necklace tossed into the forest. Canoeists first take a larger excursion boat on Columbia Lake, chug through Long Lake, and eventually arrive at the mouth of Crystal River, where they pick up their smaller two-person craft. A canoeing expedition takes about three hours and is not recommended for kids under six years, although older kids could easily make the trip. The Crystal meanders east and south through bright green timberland and Holstein-filled pastures to conclude at a pickup location. Don't worry about being abandoned; contemporary voyageurs are always rescued by a bus that will take them back to their cars. Ding's is found by taking State

Highway 22 to Waupaca County Q. Then go east about 3 miles. Ding's is open daily from April through mid-October, generally from 10:00 A.M. to 2:30 P.M.

For some indoor fun **Indian Crossings Casino and Entertainment Center** is also located at Ding's Dock. Originally a dance hall, the old roadhouse used to feature touring big bands during the 'They Shoot Horses' era of the 1920s and 1930s. Today, after a canoe excursion, visitors wolf down burgers and fries and play pinball. Through the summer teen dances are held at least twice a month, with live bands or DJs. Call Ding's for details.

WAUSAU

Originally called Big Bull Falls, Wausau had its name changed in 1850 when a local businessman thought the Indian term for "far away" had a more exotic ring than its former handle. This Marathon County city went into its adolescence in Wisconsin's logging boom that followed the Civil War. Today with its paper factories, shopping malls, and recreational opportunities, it is one of the major metropolitan areas of northern Wisconsin. While those 150 years or so of urban growth may seem impressive, consider the surrounding geologic landscape. **Rib Mountain,** which overlooks the city on its west side, is estimated to be a billion years old. Surviving the crunch of the Ice Age, which flattened most of the neighborhood under its refrigerator grip, the mountain remains the third highest point in the state, at 1,940 feet. Only 12 feet behind the front runner (Timm's Hill in nearby Price County), Rib Mountain is still tops for the longest downhill ski runs in the upper Midwest. An observation tower at the peak provides an amazing look for miles around, one where the kids can almost see forever on a clear day. The mountain is now a state park (715–842–2522), with camping, hiking, and mountain biking, along with winter skiing. Take Highway 51 to County Highway N to the park entrance. A state park sticker is required.

Wausau's **Artrageous Weekend,** held in early September, features a Festival of Arts on the downtown pedestrian mall. More than a hundred juried artists represent a variety of media, from glass to graphics and everything in between. Many of the artists demonstrate their production processes. There is also a hands-on area for children, giving them the chance to "throw" a pot, paint, and work with clay. There is no need to go hungry either, because dozens of local restaurants and ethnic organizations set up booths along the brick and tree-lined mall, serving everything from the standard burger to more exotic fare from the Far East, Latin America, and Europe.

For more information on the Artrageous Weekend, contact the Wausau Area Convention and Visitors Bureau, Box 6190, Wausau 55402–6190 (800–236–9728).

The area around Wausau provides excellent mountain-biking opportunities for daredevil dads, moms, and kids. **Nine-Mile Recreation Area** on Red Bud Road off County Highway N is a maze of logging roads that double as mountain bike paths in the summer and cross-country ski runs in the winter. None of the paths are marked only for bikers, so riders should be aware of hikers as well. So, whether by foot or pedal power, the dips and ridges of the heavily forested rec region are challenging . . . especially in the mud, which the kids will absolutely love! Trail maps are necessary to prevent becoming lost. To obtain a copy, contact the Marathon County Forestry Department, 500 Forest Street, Wausau 55401 (715–847–5267).

The best place in Marathon County for a leisurely picnic is the **Dells of the Eau Claire,** a park 11 miles east of the city on County Highway N to County Y. The term *dells* does not refer to "the farmer in the . . . " but is a corruption of the French word *dalles,* meaning "gorge." Ancient volcanic rock there was eroded by the Eau Claire River over the eons to form fantastic shapes. Several hiking trails through the park eventually lead to the river, which still bubbles and foams around the base of the massive stones. One of the paths leads over a dam from the forest on the south side of the river to a camping/swimming area on the north. No swimming is recommended below the dam because of the rocks and the current. In fact, signs warn of the danger, so stick to the approved dunking site well upriver. Potholes in the cliffs, formed by rocks swirled around by glacial runoff, can be seen along the riverbanks festooned with wildflowers.

In the winter the region is a skiing paradise. As mentioned, the Nine-Mile Recreation Area is tops, with 19 miles of loops kicking off from a ski lodge that offers rentals and instructions (715–693–5844). Season and day passes are required. **Big Eau Pleine Park Trail** loops for 7 miles on machine-set double tracks on a peninsula of a county park of the same name. Take State Highway 153, 7½ miles west of Highway 51 (the Mosinee exit). Turn south on Big Eau Pleine Park Road and follow it 3½ miles to the park entrance. Continue in the park 1 mile to a parking area on the left side.

The **Sylvan Hill/American Legion Trail** is frequently groomed and adequate for beginners and intermediates. The lane swoops along the hills of the American Legion Golf Course hills, located on the northeast side of Wausau. Drive North Sixth Street (which is actually Marathon County Highway W) to Golf Club Road or to Horseshoe Spring Road and turn right (east). Parking lots are available there at the chalet or the American Legion clubhouse.

WAUTOMA

Kid-size horses graze in the fields at the **MH Ranch,** homestead of **McHugh's Miniature Horses** (608–296–2171), on County Y just off State Highway 22 in Wautoma. McHugh's has some one hundred tiny horses, none of which exceed 34 inches in height. Subsequently, equestrian-minded tykes can almost see eye to eye with the miniatures. When born, the horses weigh only about 13 pounds and are 13 inches high. An exhibit hall shows off the dozens of trophies the horses have won in shows around the country. It is best to call ahead to inquire about tours because the ranch did not offer them in 1995, although drive-by viewing of the miniature horses, however, is always encouraged.

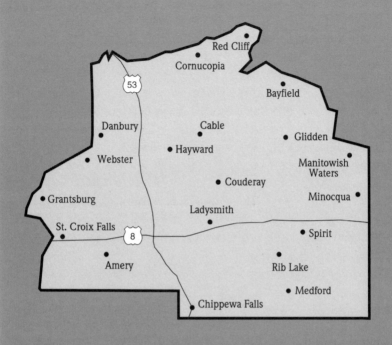

Red Cliff

Cornucopia

53

Bayfield

Danbury

Cable

Glidden

Hayward

Webster

Manitowish
Waters

Couderay

Grantsburg

Minocqua

Ladysmith

St. Croix Falls

8

Spirit

Amery

Rib Lake

Medford

Chippewa Falls

North-Northwest

NORTH-NORTHWEST

Wisconsin is a rough-and-ready place in its far northwest corner. The Ice Age molded the landscape as would a chef with a rolling pin and tossed boulders around like raisins on a soda bread crust. The area was comparatively late to be settled; loggers and farmers came into the area permanently only around the turn of the century. Subsequently, this part of the Badger State still has a raw—yet friendly—tinge to it. You know you aren't far from frontier days when deer roam casually across highways and bears and wolves are occasionally spotted in the deep forests.

Of course, families don't need to pack peanut butter and jelly survival sandwiches to head into the St. Croix River Valley or touch the frosty rim of Lake Superior. There are ski chalets here that put the Swiss mountains in the back row. There are vibrant arts programs and theaters that sparkle with the professionalism of an evening in Paris. But there is no denying that this section of the state is an outdoor lover's paradise. Cross-country skiing, snowmobiling, hiking, camping, hunting, and fishing are bread and butter words to the folks who live here and the guests who visit.

Pause at a scenic overlook. Show the kids by your example that it takes but a minute to gaze over the maples and pines to get back in touch with the better part of yourself. Now that's the basis for a good vacation.

AMERY

Stop at **Willowbrook Farms** (715–268–7053) in Amery for a peek into how sheep's milk is used to make cheese. Willowbrook's dairy is one of the first in the United States to use sheep's milk for its Deronda, Queso Fresco, Ewezarella, Golden Kaas, and Dorset Romano varieties. Tastings are allowed. Dairying, as well as lamb, wool, and breeding stock production, keeps the Koller family busy on their farms. Visitors are always welcome, with youngsters really getting into petting the spring lambs. A little gift shop there has "ewenique" gifts. The farm is located on Polk County Highway 65, 10 miles east of Amery, and is open year-round. Since this is a working farm, it is best to call ahead to arrange a free tour.

No one needs to be sheepish when driving the bumper cars at **Mini Meadows** (715–268–7143), at 911 Lincoln Avenue in Amery. An admission fee is charged. Kids and grownups can bump 'em. And dodge 'em. And crash, thump, bang, and slam 'em. Just watch out for the sheriff's car, complete with its flashing red warning lights as it swirls around the floor. Of course, nobody will actually be "pulled over" and ticketed. Simply hang on for any subsequent bump-and-bang collision. The Meadows course has 1,900 square feet of driving area, making it one of the largest car courts in the state's northwest. The facility also has eighteen of the toughest minigolf holes in this neck of the woods. Try to get through a 3-inch telephone pole to make a phone ring. But don't get hung up in traffic because of the road construction area on Hole No. 6. Putt through the jukebox on Hole No. 8 to hear wild renditions of 1950s and 1960s music.

For vacationing little people the Little People exhibit at Mini Meadows is just their size. The 30-foot-long display was made in Australia in the 1920s and consists of 7-inch-high carved wooden figures. Bringing the characters to life is a long shaft with pulleys, gears, springs, and other behind-the-scenes technicalities that are powered by a one-half-horsepower electric motor. Eyes blink, arms move, potatoes are peeled, fiddlers fiddle, and on and on. Also here are Santa's Toy Mine, the Army Camp, Touring Cars, Pixies' Workshop, and Nursery Rhyme Land.

Mini Meadows is open daily from late May through Labor Day and weekends through early October.

BAYFIELD

The gateway to the **Apostle Islands National Lakeshore,** Bayfield seems to be the end of the world. In a way it is, tucked high atop the rim of northern Wisconsin where the freezing green waters of Lake Superior lap at its ankles. Twenty-one of the Apostles are just offshore. They are mere smudges on the horizon when viewed from boat docks at the foot of a hill on which most of the village perches. I recall a gentle August shower one time that freshened what had been a humid, dog-day afternoon. Leaving the dry comfort of a nearby little restaurant, the hamburger-and-apple-pie-stuffed kids and I strolled down to the water's edge to sit on a white park bench (never minding the resulting damp behinds). A brilliant rainbow jumped from the lake to seemingly leapfrog from island to island. Everyone agreed the sight was better than a laser show, promoting demands to immediately venture forth to find the buried pirate treasures that must be out there. Being the perfect father, I naturally turned the discussion to the visual treasure just offshore. Probably not quite totally convincing, but it quieted the chatter.

Once a commercial fishing village, Bayfield is now home to guest houses and restaurants, with apple orchards and raspberry farms in the surrounding farmlands. The largest grower in the state, Einar Olson, left Milwaukee's urban rush a number years ago with his family. They took over a farm and began growing berries and harvesting apples. After two decades of love and sweat, he now ships his product around the upper Midwest, with his **Bayfield Orchards** apple jam being a prime lip-smacker. Tours of the orchards are available. In spring the trees are a blaze of white blossoms, with a sweet, precider fragrance permeating the gentle air.

The orchards (715–779–3637) are located on Betzold Road between Bayfield County Highways 1 and 3. The best time to come is in the spring to smell the wonderful scent of apple blossoms. Harvest time in the autumn is also perfect for a visit; call ahead to check when the harvest is in and ready to munch.

The village is named after Admiral Henry Bayfield, who surveyed Lake Superior between 1823 and 1825. Its prime location quickly made it a favored harbor for fishing fleets. Summer visitors from the Twin Cities,

Milwaukee, and Chicago then added their own flavor over the generations. Several of Bayfield's Victorian-era mansions, such as the fabled **Rittenhouse Inn** (715–779–5111), have been reopened as country inns or B&B facilities. The Rittenhouse is noted for its table-groaning meals featuring fresh products from the neighborhood. It is located at 301 Rittenhouse Avenue, on a hill overlooking the city. The view of the town and lake is great, regardless of the season. But a quiet summertime perch on the front porch puts all of Wisconisn's North Country life into a calm perspective. The twenty elegantly appointed private rooms range from $99 to $189.

Several of the inns and homes are now listed on the National Register of Historic Places. Families are generally welcome; just don't let the toddlers climb up the chintz curtains or swing from the crystal chandeliers.

After exploring Bayfield, take the time to visit the Apostles, with Madeline Island being a prime destination. Sailors love the wind and freshwater action around all the rocky, fir-crowned pinnacles. The Apostles got their name from early settlers who obviously couldn't count but had a bibli-

Kayakers can appreciate the rugged scenery (and maybe spot a lighthouse) at Lake Superior's Apostle Islands. (Courtesy Laughlin/Constable, Inc. & Wisconsin Division of Tourism)

cal sense of nomenclature. Instead of only twelve, there are actually twenty-two islands in the chain. Sailboats add colorful dashes during the season. Regattas and races are held throughout the summer, with entrants scooting across the lake like waterbugs.

One of the most exciting trips of my several to Madeline Island was a 5:00 A.M. snowmobile expedition across the frozen waters of Lake Superior. The jaunt, part of a 400-mile run along the tip-top of the state, took place on a crisp, thirty-five-degrees-below-zero predawn several years ago. Following a trail marked by old Christmas trees, our convoy of sleds scooted the 3 dark miles from Bayfield across the creaking, groaning ice to La Pointe. Everything was in hard relief; the cold seemed to have frozen the world in its tracks. The stars were mere stabs of light overhead. Lost in our own thoughts, protected by helmet, leather suits, and gloves, we hit the beach and toured the shuttered town and hibernating island for two hours before heading back to Bayfield for breakfast.

Generally, however, when spring brings the thaw, Madeline is reached via an easier, twenty-minute ride aboard one of the vessels belonging to the **Madeline Island Ferry Line** (715–747–2051). The ferry leaves on the half hour daily in the summer and every hour to hour and a half in the winter. Ticket prices for each vehicle vary from $4.75 to $6.75 with a $3.00 fee for each adult. The dock is on Washington Avenue. Kids can act as jolly tars, catching the spray from the bow and letting the wind tousle their hair on the ride over. Just watch out for screeching seagulls and their dive-bombed droppings.

The freshness of late spring is the best time for wandering the streets, poking for shells, and dropping by the **Madeline Island Historical Museum** in La Pointe. Housed in four historic buildings and an information center, the museum traces the community from its pre-European days to contemporary times. La Pointe itself, along with Green Bay and Prairie du Chien, is one of the three oldest white settlements in Wisconsin, dating to the 1600s and 1700s, when the first French voyageurs set up their encampments.

The museum was founded by Leo Casper and his artist wife, Isabella, two longtime summer visitors to the island whose home was actually in St. Paul. They opened the facility in 1958 and gave it to the State Historical

Society in 1968. The building is open May 28 through October 2. There is a fee. For information contact the Madeline Island Historical Museum, La Pointe 54850 (715–747–2415).

Madeline Island Bus Tours (715–747–2051) can be picked up at the La Pointe ferry dock if you don't have a car or bike or if you prefer not to walk. The tours operate April through December. After that it's snow-shoes, skis, or snowmobiles. Tickets for age twelve and older are $6.75, while children ages six to eleven can ride for $3.75. Children ages five and under ride for free.

CABLE

One section of the 47-kilometer **American Birkebeiner** cross-country ski racetrack between Cable and Hayward (a community just to the south in Sawyer County) is used in the summer by hikers and mountain bikers. Birkie details can be obtained by calling (800) 872–2753 (national) or (800) 722–3386 (Wisconsin). Later in the year hundreds of bikers enter the Chequamegon Fat Tire Bike Race and Festival. No Pee-Wee Herman bikers, these hardy souls pound over the rugged landscape to demonstrate that hardy calves and thighs can do wonders in the woods on their chunky, rugged bikes. The race begins at Telemark Lodge in Cable, and ten food sta-tions along the trail offer a bite to eat and a place to cheer on one's favorite biker.

But park your bikes outside the **Cable Natural History Museum** (715–798–3890), at County M and Randysek Road, for an impressive tour of stuffed and mounted regional wildlife and other nature exhibits. The museum, which is open at no charge, also offers hands-on field trips into the surrounding countryside for a special look at all the rich flora and fauna. Lectures and workshops are held throughout the year, many of them geared to youngsters. The facility is open only from 10:00 A.M. to 4:00 P.M. Tuesdays through Saturdays. It is an important facility to visit in order to help kids understand what makes nature tick.

Snowmobiling is great fun in **Chequamegon National Forest,** with clubs helping to keep up the trail system. The Sno-Drifters, Black River Rock Dodgers, Northwoods Riders Snowmobile Club, Medford Stump

Jumpers, Jump River Runners, Pine Creek Riders, Moonlite Sno-Kats, Westboro Sno-Dusters, and Interwald Wanderers are among the many that ensure quality riding. These are family-based groups, with moms, dads, and kids participating.

Entire communities support the tourism effort in these forest areas. For instance, Perkinstown (west of Medford) is called the hub of winter recreation in Taylor County, because of the **Perkinstown Winter Sports Area.** The park is complete with a cozy chalet, where outdoors folks can find a fireplace and nibble food. Kids will love tubing down the snow-covered hills in the park. There are both rope tows and stairs for them to get back to the ridge peaks. The tubing rates are $3.00 for children ages six to eleven, $4.00 for kids up to age seventeen, and $5.00 for adults; cross-country skiing is free. The facility is located on Winter Sports Road off Highway 64 just 11 miles west of Medford. Hours are 11:00 A.M. to 5:00 P.M. Saturday and Sunday and 5:00 to 9:00 P.M. Friday evenings. For more information call (715) 785–7722.

CHIPPEWA FALLS

Chippewa Falls once had the world's largest sawmill under one roof—**Chippewa Log and Boom, Inc.,** built by Irvin Warehowser and his partner, lawyer Edward Rutledge, in the 1870s. Harvested from the surrounding forests, white and red pine with trunks several feet in diameter were sliced, diced, and chawed by the ripping blades to produce tens of thousands of board feet of lumber a year. The old mill is now history, just a memory in this town that was once a hub of the state's lumber world.

Fun for the family can be had at the **Jacob Leinenkugel Brewing Company** (715–723–5557), 1–3 Jefferson Avenue, where tours of the brewery and samples in the Hospitality Center make a rainy vacation day much more pleasant . . . or, for that matter, a steamy summer afternoon . . . or a cheerful spring morning . . . or a raw autumn noontime. While the folks can tip a brewskie, sodas are available for kids, who will have just learned about the High Trinity of Brewing: malt, mash, and wort. Jake Leinenkugel, the fourth-generation family member in the business, is proud to head the city's oldest business, established in 1867. Ol' Jake portrays a down-home type of guy in his company's ads, belying the fact that the forty-ish brewmeister is a savvy businessman who eased his firm through a potentially rocky buyout by Miller Brewing Company in the 1980s. Leinenkugel managed to keep his hand in the brewery operations.

The brewery gift shop is open Monday through Friday from 9:00 A.M. to 5:00 P.M. and Sunday from 9:00 A.M. to 4:00 P.M. Summer tours are held daily between 9:30 A.M. and 3:30 P.M. From Labor Day to June 1, tours are scheduled at 11:00 A.M. and 1:30 P.M. Monday through Friday only. There is no charge.

After a pleasant pause over a Leinie's, it is now time again to treat the kids. Take the chillun to **Irvine Park** (715–723–3890) on Bridgewater Avenue for a tour of the zoo there, with its excellent and exotic assortment of fangs, hooves, claws, and horns, none of which will be seen on neighboring farms. It is open year-round from morning until dark. There is no admission charge.

After admiring the bears, lions, and other beasts, take a dip in the park's outdoor swimming pool for another cool-off opportunity. There are also 300 acres of woodland for camping (for a fee) and hiking. In December the city sets up a Christmas Village in the park, draping upward of 30,000 brightly colored lights over the trees. There are also seventy-five individual Victorian holiday displays spotted around the park, accessible by driving the roads that wend their way between the firs. With the splash of light playing across the snow—and it always snows in Chippewa Falls in December—mayoral fiat, I guess—the effect is mind-expanding. Then tumble back to a local nearby restaurant for hot chocolate.

CORNUCOPIA

State Highway 13 skirts the underbelly of frosty Lake Superior, that ship-eating pond laying claim to being the world's largest body of fresh water. The lake is 350 miles long and 160 miles wide, covering 31,820 square miles, of which 20,620 are in the United States. The average depth is 475 feet. That's a lot of H_2O. Even usually jaded teens can gaze at all those green-black waves and stand in awe. The tiny towns of Cornucopia, Herbster, and Port Wing offer lakeshores for strolling and deepwater charter fishing for monster lake salmon and German brown trout for a Captain Ahab/Moby-Dick feel.

Cornucopia is Wisconsin's northernmost village, a mere sneeze in size, tucked as it is into Siskiwit Bay. But the town does boast a small private airport. The onion-shaped dome of **St. Mary's Greek Orthodox Church** doesn't seem out of place, a central gathering place several generations ago when a contingent of Greek fisherfolk first moved to the area. The building is located on Wisconsin Highway 13 in the center of the one-highway town. For more information about the church, call (715) 742–3232. A wayside just off the highway in the heart of town is a perfect spot to pull over and picnic. Since it is usually breezy in these parts, be sure someone in the family is in charge of retrieving lost napkins. This is a good job for the under-seven set when they tire of skipping flat stones across the watery deep.

Just to the east of Amnicon Falls is the small town of **Poplar,** home of Richard Bong, the Army Air Corps' leading ace of World War II, with forty confirmed kills in the Pacific Theater. The **Bong Memorial** in town includes an authentic P-38 fighter plane. It is located on School Road, adjacent to the Popular Elementary School, 1 block north of Main Street. For information about Richard Bong, write Box 326, Poplar 54864 (715–364–2553).

COUDERAY

Whenever Windy City gangster Al Capone needed a break from breaking the law, he would head to the Wisconsin North Woods for a little R&R, leading his convoy of limos and gun-toting pals. Not that criminal activity is glorified at the **Hideout** (715–945–2746) in Couderay, but the spot has a definite place in the state's history. Capone and his cronies stayed at the lodge on a regular basis, to fish, play cards, tell FBI jokes, and get in some target practice. Stone outbuildings are well settled into the woodsy landscape like squat, undersize castles, but at least one taller structure is reputed to be a watchtower. Not that anyone bothered Scarface on his visits— the locals always made a wide berth around the lodge when he arrived. The Hideout is now a steakhouse, offering some of the best meals and best gangster ghosts this side of Chicago's Michigan Avenue. The kids should be impressed by the rumors of secret cellars that allegedly hid Prohibition booze. They'll be wide-eyed about the legends of long-deceased dandies in double-breasted threads who carried violin cases but couldn't play a tune. Just remind the youngsters to pay their taxes, since it was such a little over-sight that did in the famed criminal. The complex is located on County CC, some 2 miles north, off State Highway 70. The Hideout is open daily mid-May to mid-September and Friday through Sunday mid-September to mid-October, noon to 7:00 P.M. Tickets are $5.00 for adults and $2.50 for children ages six to eleven.

DANBURY

The unincorporated village of Danbury on State Highway 77 is the trail-head for the 50-mile **Gandy Dancer Trail,** which was opened in 1990. Called a silent trail because motorized vehicles cannot use it (except for ATVs and snowmobiles in the winter), the trail will eventually be black-topped. Now it is primarily a mountain-bike route that travels along an old railroad line track from the Minnesota border near Danbury southward to St. Croix Falls in Polk County. The rugged route travels mostly through the scenic wilderness, passing close to towns but far enough away to provide a real sense of adventure. But as one resident indicated, bikers have a ten-dency to run into trees. So the community has outfitted an ambulance with tracks that can be hauled by truck to the trailhead. The rescue vehicle can then churn its way into the woods. Since the trail traverses remote areas of the county, riders are admonished not to ride alone, in case of emergencies. This is something to consider when taking smaller children out on the trail.

Bed-and-breakfast inns near the Gandy Dancer accept tired, foot-weary youngsters, as do motels and hotels throughout the region. But pets are seldom welcome. To confirm what takes who, check the free *Burnett County Resort and Campground Guide* (for a copy call 800–788–3164). One of the B&Bs, **Forgotten Tymes Country Inn** (715–349–5837), on Tower Road in Siren, is on 133 acres of prime wilderness land where kids can run and yell to their hearts' content. The ten guest rooms are in century-old log cabins that are handicapped accessible. Innkeepers Al and

Pat Blume turn out a hearty breakfast as well. A family of four can spend a night in the cabins for only $145.

The land near Danbury was let out for homesteading as late as 1900, demonstrating that life on the Wisconsin frontier is not so far removed from the minds of Burnett County residents. Donna Nelson, a secretary in the county's tourism office, recalls that her Swedish father-in-law, Johan Nelson, was a tote driver who brought all food, mail, and kerosene by horse-drawn wagon to the local folks. It took a whole day to drive the 35 miles from the supply center at Grantsburg to Danbury. Tell that to the teens who want a car to drive to school 3 blocks away! When the railroad came through the community in 1912, however, the link to the outside world was solidified.

GLIDDEN

The sprawling timberland of the **Chequamegon National Forest** is prime camping area for anyone from the novice to the highly motivated, experienced backpacker. Even kids can have an adventure deep inside the thousands of square miles of pine, maple, poplar, and sumac that make up the U.S. Forest Service's **Glidden District** (715–762–2461). Adventurous four-wheel driving is part of the fun on old logging trails and gravel roads, where grazing moose can be spotted in foggy predawn hours. And yes, there are bears there. Not the teddy bear "Dancing with Uncle Walter" folk-song bears but honest-to-gosh hungry bears.

Glidden, located between the towns of Butternut and Mellen, calls itself the Black Bear Capital of the World and offers a reward for anyone bringing in a bigger beast than the 665-pounder that was shot near town in 1963. That bear is now stuffed and displayed in a glass-enclosed case near one of the downtown gas stations. The bear was so big it had to be weighed on the lumberyard scales. Exiting Wisconsin Highway 13 on Main Street, drive past the lumberyard and straight up the hill where the bruin can be spotted in all his stuffed ferocity.

So who would want to take kids into a place where large, toothy animals in raggedy coats meander? It's an easy question to answer. Anyone who enjoys the outdoors will find the forestland a great place for hiking, camping, fishing, and hunting, regardless of age. And the bears—well, they generally stay out of sight and out of mind. Campers should just hang food high in a tree or keep it locked in a car trunk overnight, well out of reach of busy paws. These precautions are no different from what a wise parent does to protect the contents of the home refrigerator when a son's high school football team comes to visit. Bears will leave campers alone who leave them alone.

GRANTSBURG

Much of Burnett County was settled by tough yet sauna-loving Scandinavians who appreciated the rugged Burnett County countryside, which reminded them of home. Many went into the logging industry. Subsequently, Norwegian, Danish, and Swedish influences are still strong throughout the region, with more guys in hunting jackets nicknamed Swede than probably anywhere else in Wisconsin. And many of the churches in Grantsburg still stage *lutfisk* suppers as fund-raisers. Vacationing kids will find these fjord feasts much more exotic than a drive-in's standard double Whopper.

Kokt lutfisk is actually dried cod that has been preserved in lye and soda and softened into a glutenous mass by letting it sit in salt water for about a week. It is then boiled and served with a white sauce *(mjolksds)*, along with boiled potatoes. Everything is liberally dosed with salt and white and black pepper. *Lefsa,* a rolled and sugared pancake, is the typical side dish. After gobbling the slithery, sliding cod concoction, try a culinary geography quiz. Tell the tykes that Madison, Wisconsin's state capital, also asserts that it is the *Lutfisk* Capital of the United States. Grantburgians, however, certainly could lay claim to that title.

For the times and dates of these suppers, check the area's newspapers: the *Inter-County Leader,* published in Frederick in adjacent Polk County, and the *Burnett County Sentinel,* published in Grantsburg. The weeklies can be picked up at grocery stores, gas stations, bait shops, and other outlets. Out-of-town vacationers are encouraged to drop by for sample papers.

The unfenced **Crex Meadows Wildlife Area** (715–463–2899) is located at the intersection of Burnett County highways D and F, ½ mile north of Grantsburg. The free facility is open to the public twenty-four hours a day. Visitors can drive around any of the good trunk roads throughout the preserve, which has a 2,399-acre bird refuge in the center. Nearly 300 acres have been cultivated to provide feed for the huge flocks of ducks and geese that call the place home. It is estimated that more than 20,000 birds at a time fly in and out of the refuge on any given day. Once-rare sandhill cranes, which zoom in from the horizon like small airplanes, have made a strong comeback within the safety of the preserve. Kids can identify these gangly birds by their high-pitched screeches, which sound like a card party of witches. Roads and observation points around the preserve allow good "birding." Bring binoculars for close-up watching. A Department of Natural Resources office is staffed year-round on weekdays from 7:45 A.M. to 4:30 P.M., but the workers are often out in the field, so it may be closed at any given time. On weekends in spring and fall, however, volunteers are on hand during the day to answer questions about the migrating flocks. April, May, June, September, and October are the peak times of feather fluttering at Crex Meadows.

HAYWARD

Hayward is one of the state's best all-year launching points for families on a vacation fun quest. Located on State Highway 77, the city is a getaway hub amid deep-blue lakes and emerald green pine forests. Stock up on groceries, wash campfire-smudged jeans, take in a movie after a television-bereft week in the woods, visit souvenir shops to purchase the requisite T-shirts and postcards, grab a real restaurant meal following days of beans and burned eggs in the bush.

In Hayward everyone from the Common Council to the gas station attendant talks fish: perch, trout, walleye, crappies. Who caught what, what bait was used, what about the water temps, who swamped their canoe while netting a monster. After all, the hundreds of bumper stickers seen around town point out that a bad day of fishing is better than a good day at work. In cafes, on street corners, in the sport shops, there's only fish, fish, fish. And speaking of fish stories, what must be the most fabulous dream experienced by any angler can be seen leaping over the oaks on the drive into Hayward. A giant muskie, the sharp-toothed monster fish of 1,000 casts, rears high on the horizon, mouth agape and glass-fiber scales flashing in the sun. Landlocked and not real, the four-story creation is the main feature of the **National Freshwater Fishing Hall of Fame** (715–634–4440).

Take the kids into the muskie-shaped museum to show off its mind-boggling displays of homemade and commercial lures, antique outboard motors, and photos of grinning guys and gals posing with their record catches. To reach the mouth of the muskie, you meander up an incline past awards, memorabilia, and trophies marking the biggest this-and-that of the finny world. One wonders what a worm would think of all this. But the question probably never crosses the minds of numerous brides who bring their newly landed husbands to the muskie maw for wedding portraits. "Smile. You can go fishing right after we're done" is a common refrain. Giant-size bluegills and bass bound out of the grass in front of the museum, with a rowboat anchored in the cement there. It's a great place for gag photos, with the children aboard facing the leaping concrete fish.

Visitors can stand in the jaws of a four-story-high muskie at the National Fresh Water Fishing Hall of Fame. (Courtesy Laughlin/Constable, Inc. & Wisconsin Division of Tourism)

The Hall of Fame is open from mid-April to November 1, 10:00 A.M. to 5:00 P.M. daily. Admission is $4.00 for adults, $2.50 for ages eleven to eighteen, and $1.50 for kids ten and under.

The facility is free but donations are requested. It is open year-round on Mondays, Wednesdays, Fridays and Saturdays from 10:00 A.M. to 2:00 P.M. Easy to find, the museum is close to US Highway 51 on the city's south side. Look for a clock tower above the building (the clock is turned off during the winter months to protect its workings).

Hayward is also the starting point for the **American Birkebeiner,** the highest-rated cross-county ski race in North America. Held each February, the Birkie hosts 8,000 to 10,000 skiers for the tortuous, 47-mile course over slopes and flatlands between Hayward and Cable, to the north in Douglas County. Norway, Sweden, Finland, Germany, Austria, and France have been among the nations represented, along with a plethora of sleekly attired Canadians and Yankees. There are various legs of the event for skiers of different skills, but each section puts physical demands on participants that are unequaled in any other race on the continent. Yet there are heats for kids, as well as oldsters. So the Birkie makes a fine, albeit exhausting, winter weekend for any family that loves challenges.

For race watchers the best spot is right downtown, where the pack takes off along the jammed main street. Bring a stepladder or a periscope to peer over the heads of the watching crowd . . . and, of course, dress for the weather. Heavy socks and waterproof boots are de rigueur for anyone standing around in the below-freezing temperatures. Then there are mittens, scarves, stocking caps, jackets, pants, ski masks, and all the other high-fashion garb that rounds out a winter in the North Woods. But it's well worth it, especially if participating.

For registration information contact the race headquarters at 110 Main, Box 911, Hayward 54843 (715–634–5025 or 800–722–3386 in Wisconsin; 800–872–2753 nationwide).

LADYSMITH

Winter doesn't mean a vacationer needs to lose perspective about Wisconsin. So what if the drifts pile up throughout the glacially formed countryside of Rusk County. So what if the weather is frosty. It's the time when the snowmobiles and cross-country skis, followed by family games in front of the fireplace, take the edge off Old Man Winter's threats. There are more than 250 miles of snowmobile trails throughout the region, with a wildly wonderful panorama of dazzling snow and ice. Some of the best power sledding is through the Blue Hills, which once constituted a 20,000-foot-high mountain range but were smushed by the grinding action of glaciers several eons ago. The **Five State Corridor Trails** go through Ladysmith to every corner of Rusk County.

For a complete listing of trails contact the Rusk County Information Center, 817 West Miner Avenue Northwest, Ladysmith 54848 (800–535–7875).

MANITOWISH WATERS

For some reason, in the 1920s and 1930s gangsters from Chicago used to enjoy Wisconsin's North Woods. The rustic lifestyle, woods, and lakes were probably considered great for R&R after a day of bank robberies, auto chases, and bootlegging. Sometimes, however, their holidays were interrupted by the fellows in the white hats. At **Little Bohemia** (715–543–8433), 2 miles south of Manitowish Waters on U.S. Highway 51, John Dillinger and his buddies were relaxing over a card game when they were ambushed in 1934 by feds and local police. Bullet holes can still be seen in the walls of a cabin beside the restaurant, hidden in the forest along Highway 51. Some of the gang's memorabilia is on display there. One local man was killed in the shoot-out, and most of the thugs and their molls escaped into the brush despite the hail of gunfire. Today's restaurant serves thick steaks, homemade soups, and hot bread right out of the oven. Just check out the fellows at the next table. The restaurant is closed in the winter months and reopens in mid-April. Meals are served then from 4:00 to 11:00 P.M. until Memorial Day, when hours are extended from 11:00 A.M. to 11:00 P.M. through Labor Day. It is closed Wednesday.

MEDFORD

Taylor County Rodeo Days (715–678–2282) in Medford brings bull riding and calf roping to northern Wisconsin, with real ranchhands trying to maintain their seats in the saddle. The traditional early June weekend includes horse sales, pony races, and plenty of country-western music after the riding. Open team penning, whereby quarterhorses get to show their training, brings cattle and cowpersons (lots of women ride too!) into close contact. The event is sanctioned by the International Professional Rodeo Association and is the richest IPRA rodeo in the United States in June, with thousands of dollars in purse money for winners. The rodeo is held at the county fairgrounds at the intersection of Highways 13 and 64.

MINOCQUA

Minocqua couldn't be much farther north or it would sneeze itself into Vilas County. For good reason it is nicknamed the Island City, for it is surrounded by 2,000 acres of water. There are more than 3,000 lakes, ponds, and puddles in the immediate vicinity. As such, this is a land (waterlogged at that) tailor-made for outdoor recreation opportunities. But a motorist doesn't need a rowboat to get to Minocqua. US Highway 51 leads right to the heart of the tourist town.

Of course, with all that water, anything wet is all right. There are dozens of boat launches, where anglers, water skiers, and swimmers have a field day. A kid can stay wrinkled all summer. The town offers free water-ski shows by the **Min A Qua Bats** each afternoon throughout the summer, with a semipro troupe of brilliantly smiling, leggy beauties who certainly earned their water wings. They flip, fly, twirl, and turn on two skis, one ski, and no skis in an exciting display that keeps even the most jaded teen interested. To get to the show area on Lake Minocqua from U.S. Highway 51, cross the first bridge over the lake. Turn immediately left on Park Street. You will find the bleachers between Bosacki's Boathouse Restaurant and the Thirsty Whale Bar. For show times call (715) 356–2220 or (715) 356–1754.

For booted landlubbers, the city is also at the tail end of the **Bearskin State Trail,** built on 19 miles of an abandoned railroad bed and taking hikers and bikers through truly scenic countryside. The trail can be picked up behind the post office. For more information on what to expect along the Bearskin, contact the trail offices at 4125 County M, Boulder Junction (715–385–2727).

Jim Peck's Wildwood–Wildlife Park (715–356–5588), on State Highway 70 just west of Minocqua, is a family place, one where it is OK to pet a raccoon, give a bearhug to a fuzzy llama, or feed the deer—all verboten in the real wilderness. But Peck has been a staple stopover in the city for years and is open daily May through mid-October 9:00 A.M. to 5:30 P.M. Prices are $5.90 for adults and $3.90 for children twelve and under. For more animal connections, the **Northwoods Wildlife Center,** 8683 Blumstein Road (715–356–7400), is a hospital for wounded critters. Injured animals can be brought to the shelter for rest, recuperation, and a friendly hand before being returned to the wilds. A visit is free, but donations are suggested. Call for appointments.

RED CLIFF

Three miles north of the village of Bayfield is the **Red Cliff Indian Reservation,** ancestral home of the Red Cliff band of Lake Superior Chippewa. The reservation is reached via County K off State Highway 13. Motorists can drive through the reservation to observe the magnificent scenery. The tribe operates a modern campground for guests.

The **Buffalo Art Center** (715–779–5858) houses tribal artifacts, with regularly scheduled demonstrations of basket making throughout the summer. Traditional canoe construction, utilizing birch and other local products, is also on the agenda. Questions are encouraged. Red Cliff Bingo on the Bay is a nightly feature throughout the year. No one under eighteen is allowed in the bingo hall, however, so plan accordingly. The reservation overlooks a picturesque bend of Lake Superior where Raspberry, Oak, Sand, York, Hermit, and Basswood islands are easily seen to the east and northeast. The dots of land are part of the Apostle Islands.

RIB LAKE

Ice Age Days at Rib Lake are usually held the second weekend in August, celebrating the glaciers that once held the county in its ice-cube grip. For details on the free event, call the Rib Lake Commercial Club at (715) 427–5761. The Franzen Brothers Circus is a regular entertainment feature, but no woolly mammoths perform in the center ring . . . just your stock-in-trade Indian elephants. A mountain-bike race, a radio-controlled model airplane demonstration, bed races, a parade, a bake sale, bingo, and an all-terrain vehicle mud run are part of the fun. Even the largest family on holiday will fill their tummies at the event's Sunday chicken dinner held in the American Legion Hall.

The Ice Age Trail, following the rim of the last glaciers that covered Wisconsin, runs north to southwest through Taylor County and is well marked. The trail actually skirts downtown Rib Lake. But the city's fathers and mothers were not cool to the idea of having a hot time to celebrate the era when there was a freezer lock on the vicinity. An Ice Age prince and princess are named to host the activities.

SPIRIT

There's not much to see in downtown Spirit because it is primarily a wide spot in the road with a few homes spread along State Highway 86. But proceed 6 miles west, turn south on Price County C, and drive 1 mile to **Timm's Hill County Park** (715–339–4505), the highest point in Wisconsin. Plenty of parking is available adjacent to a picnic area and lake in the park near the actual hill. A steep trail through the thick woods leads to an observation tower crowning the 1,951½-foot peak. In getting there, take your time with little kids. Stubby legs might have a hard time scrambling upward, if there are slippery leaves and pine needles en route. But they'll love the feeling of accomplishment once they reach the base of the tower, far from the sight of autos and covered picnic shelters far below. It's a real neck-craner looking upward from the bottom of the tower, and I lost track of the number of steps to what seemed to be a cloud-tagging platform. Yet after some hundred and more steps, pausing to overcome height fears and catch the breath, a stalwart climber is rewarded with an awesome view of the surrounding countryside. The view is best in the autumn, during Colorama, when the oaks, maples, and birches burn with the season's Jack Frost fire. Be sure to take a camera to capture the quiltlike visual effect. The park is open year-round.

ST. CROIX FALLS

The 1,400-acre **Interstate Park** at St. Croix Falls presents some of the best scenic views in Wisconsin, with 100-foot-high cliffs tumbling down to the rampaging St. Croix River. The *dalles* (gorges) of the St. Croix were earmarked as the state's first state park at the turn of the century. Several trails loop through the park near the intersection of State Highways 8 and 35, directly across the river from Minnesota. For the kids one of the best routes amid the rocks is the Pothole Trail at the base of the cliffs. Numerous holes of varying sizes and depths show where glaciers tumbled stones around and around, making them as smooth as cannonballs and burrowing deep pockets into the bedrock. Regular tours are held in the summer, with the rangers providing plenty of background on geologic phenomena.

While meandering along the other paths (River Bluffs Trail, Echo Canyon Trail, Meadow Valley Trail, and Eagle Peak Trail), encourage sharp-eyed kids to identify the Old Man of the Dalles. This craggy formation, which peers out over the river, resembles a man's face. Just don't become so intent on finding the old guy that someone falls over a cliff. There are no handrails over the gorge (unlike on the Minnesota side at Taylor Falls), so keep a close watch on small climbers. Plenty of campsites in the park are available for overnight layovers; call (715) 483–3747. The visitors center is open all year, daily from 8:30 A.M. to 4:00 P.M. A state park sticker is required to walk the trails. A resident daily pass is $4.00, with a non-resident daily pass at $6.00. Resident annual passes are $15 and non-resident annual passes are $24. Motor vehicles must have an admission sticker attached to the inside of the windshield on the driver's side before parking.

The park is a key hub of the **St. Croix National Scenic Riverway**, covering 250 miles of the Namekagon and St. Croix rivers. The system was established in 1968 to keep the waters in a primitive form. A National Park

Service interpretive center (715–483–3284) is located in downtown St. Croix Falls, not far from the state park headquarters about 1 block west of Main Street alongside the rushing river. Look for the directional signage. Helpful rangers can answer questions about the Scandinavian immigrants who settled the region, the logging business, and area recreational opportunities.

If a vacationing family is in the area, it's only fair to mention Taylors Falls, directly across the St. Croix River, for more commercial fun at the **Wild Mountain Recreation Park,** located on Minnesota Highway 16, 7 miles north of Taylors Falls (800–447–4958). The facility has two 1,700-foot-long Alpine slides, bumper cars, waterslides, go-carts, and picnic areas.

The park is open daily from early May until mid-October for summer activities and during the snow season, generally December through early March. Hours are weekdays 10:00 A.M. to 10:00 P.M., Friday 10:00 A.M. to 11:00 P.M., Saturday 9:30 A.M. to 10:00 P.M., and Sunday 9:30 A.M. to 9:00 P.M.

Prices for ski-lift tickets and equipment rentals vary depending on the day of the week, time of day, and age of the skier. Call for details.

In the summer, varying rates are available for canoe rentals depending on the miles paddled. For instance, for $54.50, outdoors lovers can get one canoe, two paddles, and two life jackets for a two-day trip on the river. Wild Mountain has some 370 canoes available for use, making it one of the largest outfitters in Minnesota–Wisconsin border country. There is also a range of fees for paddleboats, waterslides, volleyball, and other activities. In addition to single-ticket prices that range from $6.95 to $9.50, unlimited ride tickets range from $8.50 to $16, depending on the activities.

WEBSTER

For 200 years, Wisconsin was one of the prime centers of the frontier fur trade. The state is dotted with old forts and cabins that once served as the economic outposts of the growing nation. Each winter, trading companies operated "wintering" posts in the wilderness. Native Americans would bring their prime pelts to these facilities and trade them for supplies. In mid-1802 a contingent of adventurers from the XY Trading Company out of Grand Portage, several hundred miles to the north in 'what eventually became Minnesota' launched their canoes and aimed south. Their mission was to service the folle avoine (wild rice) region of Wisconsin. At **Forts Folle Avoine** near Webster, they built a trading post near that of another firm, the North West Company, which had found a lucrative market there already.

The traders remained at Forts Folle Avoine for two winters, trading with the Ojibwa Indians who lived in the vicinity. Today costumed guides depict typical traders who lived at the fort during its heyday, demonstrating the principles of barter and explaining life in the forests. Other guides show off Native American craft traditions, from basket making to food preparation.

A stockade and outbuildings at the original site of Forts Folle Avoine can be toured, with plenty of information available on why things were done the way they were back in the good old days. Questions are encouraged at this hands-on re-creation of "Let's Make a Deal" woodsy style. Regularly scheduled interpretive programs are held in the evening and on weekends in two outdoor amphitheaters.

Forts Folle Avoine is reached via State Highway 35, 4 miles north of Webster to County Road U. Go west on U 2½ miles through the forest to the site, which is managed by the Burnett County Historical Society (715–349–2219). The facility is open Memorial Day through Labor Day from 9:00 A.M. to 5:00 P.M. It is closed Mondays and Tuesdays except on holidays. Admission is charged.

CENTRAL

This is where Wisconsin's action is. Cheese festivals, politics, mountain biking, face painting, museums—central Wisconsin pulls all the best parts of the state together in a grand pastiche of things to see and do. How can a family go wrong when there is a chance to milk (by hand) a cow on the front lawn of the state capitol building, yet walk 3 blocks away and see some of the best children's theater in the nation? There is no denying that liver sausage on rye, with onions, is best in Madison's university deli scene, but how about mustard? Well, take a run to nearby Mount Horeb and see for yourself how condiments can be classy. Ice cream from contented cows, sunsets out of Picasso . . . it's all there.

Central Wisconsin is a most delightful mix of backcountry roads, main streets, and magic. The urbane, smooth, and cool of the big-city scene fit well with the down-home flavor of small towns—communities that seem as if they were dropped out of Old Europe. Want to get a tattoo (ah, don't tell Junior), indulge in a gourmet meal, camp under the stars, purchase a whimsical piece of handcrafted gold jewelry?

That's all of mid-Wisconsin, the place where if somebody calls you a cheesehead, you should consider it a compliment. It means you are part of the

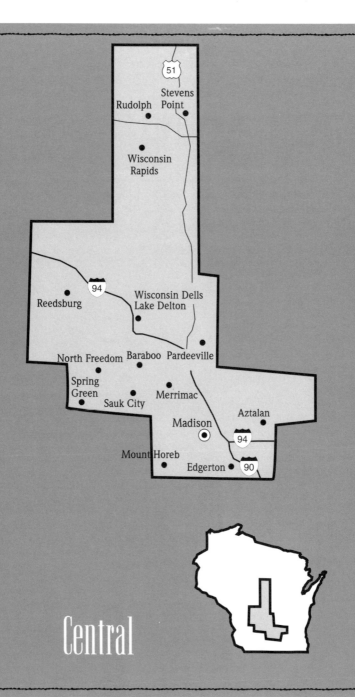

51

Stevens
Point
Rudolph

Wisconsin
Rapids

94
Reedsburg
Wisconsin Dells
Lake Delton

North Freedom Baraboo Pardeeville
Spring
Green
Sauk City Merrimac
Aztalan
Madison
94
Mount Horeb
Edgerton 90

Central

Badger State gang. And, hey, that ain't bad when you're just passin' through.

AZTALAN

In Aztalan bikers can pick up the **Glacial Drumlin Bike Trail** (314–648–8774), a 47-mile pathway of crushed rock on a former railroad bed. The trail, which runs through some of the most scenic parts of central Wisconsin, extends from Cottage Grove in the west to Waukesha in the east. It is easily ridden by cyclists of any age and is used by cross-country skiers and snowmobilers in the winter. There are plenty of places to pause along the route for restaurants, rest stops, and ice cream. In one fancy fashion gesture, the Welsh national flag flies over the trailside pit stop in the town of Wales, one of the many small communities along the route.

The eastern half of the trail starts at MacArthur Road on the west side of Waukesha. To reach the trailhead from I–94, exit State Highway 164 (which is also North Street) and go south through five stoplights to St. Paul Avenue. Turn right onto St. Paul to MacArthur Road and go right again on MacArthur for about ¼ mile. Parking is on the street; a picnic table, shelter, and water fountain are available.

The trail starts (or ends) here, extending some 25 miles to Switzke Road, just 3 miles east of Jefferson. The western half of the trail begins at Dane County Highway N, across the street from the post office in Cottage Grove, and extends to Junction Road outside Jefferson, where it crosses the sluggish Rock River.

A state pass is required to use the trail. The authorizations can be purchased for $3.00 a day or $10 a season from sports shops, gas stations, and other retail outlets along the route; "honest boxes" at rest stops; rangers who regularly patrol the pathway; and Lake Kegonsa State Park or the Lapham Peak Unit of the Kettle Moraine State Forest office. A pass is required between April 1 and October 31 for biking, mountain biking, and horseback riding and in the December-to-February winter season for skiing. The Glacial Drumlin trail is accessible to bikers, hikers, and joggers in the summer and to snowmobilers and skiers in the winter. No all-terrain vehicles are allowed, so keep the motorized three-wheelers at home. Dogs must be leashed.

For information, contact the Glacial Drumlin Trail-East, N846–W329, CTH "C," Delafield 53018 (414–646–3025) or the Glacial Drumlin Trail–West, 1213 South Main Street, Lake Mills 53551 (414–648–8774).

BARABOO

"Hold yer hosses! The elephants is comin'." The shrill cry announcing the conclusion of a circus parade was always enough to get the blood racing for anyone under thirteen years old. Today's kids don't often have that chance to feel the excitement of rising up early and racing down to the railyards to watch a show unload, then follow it to the grounds and help put up bleachers. There has always been something magical about the sawdust world.

But you can still pass along a touch of that center ring excitement to your youngsters during a visit to the **Circus World Museum** (608–356–0800), the former winter quarters of the Ringling Brothers Circus. The museum buildings are spread along Water Street, with the main entrance at 426 Water. While the museum is open year-round (Mondays through Saturdays from 9:00 A.M. to 5:00 P.M. and Sundays from 11:00 A.M. to 5:00 P.M.), shows run from early May through late September. In addition to the main headquarters number, a 24-hour information line gives the latest updates on which circus star is performing when and what new exhibits have been developed. Admission is $3.25 for adults; $2.75 for seniors 65 and over; and $1.75 for kids five through twelve.

The sprawling acreage along the sluggish Baraboo River is packed with bright red, orange, and white circus wagons dating back generations. The Ringlings were here well before they linked up with Barnum and Bailey, turning this central Wisconsin town into a place of spangles and tinsel. Many of the performers and workers lived, retired, died, and were buried here in the 1880s and 1890s. The various administration buildings and barns now house delightfully splendiferous displays of pulchritude, acrobatic skill, and uncaged ferocity. Rather like talking about your family, right? Photos, posters, and memorabilia from hundreds of artistes, clowns, and roustabouts adorn the walls and exhibition cases. Model circus wagons, intricate in their detail, will capture the attention of kids, who can view them at eye level, to say nothing of looking up at the real wagons spotted around the grounds.

Several times a day circus crews load and unload wagons from rail-cars to demonstrate how it used to be done by horses and snorting tractors. The same procedures are used when unloading the wagons in Milwaukee prior to the Great Circus Parade each summer, after their train trip from Baraboo.

On the way out of Circus World, snap a photo of the kids in the gorilla cage. No, it's not for sale for the ride home.

In downtown Baraboo at 136 Fourth Avenue, the fabulous **Al Ringling Theater,** built by the oldest of the Ringlings, is still being used. Around the town square everything seems to have a circus motif. Even the designs on the outside of the courthouse depict a circus parade. Call (608) 356–8864.

For another stop in the Baraboo area, one strictly for the birds, drop in at the **International Crane Foundation,** E11376 Shady Lane (608–356–9462). Experts in bird lore, naturalists, and avian researchers

Handlers put elephants through their paces at the Circus World Museum at Baraboo.

use the foundation facilities to study these gangly birds from Australia, China, India, and other nations. Some fifteen species are represented. It is most fun when the keepers need to act out mating routines to perk the birds' interest. To see people fluttering, hooting and hopping on one leg or the other is truly amazing. One wonders what the birds think. Whatever it is, tell the kids that it works. So the crane comes before the egg? The foundation grounds are open for self-guided strolling May 1 through October 31, 9:00 A.M. to 5:00 P.M. Guided tours are held at 10:00 A.M., 1:00 P.M., and 3:00 P.M. from Memorial Day through Labor Day and weekends in May, September, and October. Group tours can be arranged between April 15 and October 31 by appointment. Admission is $12:00 for adults (twelve and over); $4.50 for seniors (sixty-two and over); and $2.50 for children. Free parking is available.

Devil's Lake State Park (608–356–8301), the state's busiest, is located along Highway 159, midway between Tourist Town Wisconsin Dells and Circus City Baraboo. It is open year-round. Since campsites go quickly each year, be sure to call early in the spring for summer reservations. The park features 500-foot-high rock walls and a 360-acre lake. Trails meander through the park, with camping, fishing, hiking, cross-country skiing, nature exhibits, Indian mounds, and picnicking among the attractions. Be sure kids stay on the trail and don't climb where they shouldn't. Stay well away from cliffs, and keep on eye on the little ones. The nature center, just inside the main entrance, has a basement kids' room in which youngsters can learn to identify animal tracks, leaves, and other outdoorsy items. A display also relates how people have affected the environment. The Future Wisconsin Explorers program, for kids in grades four and up, is easy to enter. To become a member, youngsters just fill out an activities booklet with games such as Wildlife Bingo, Snake-Opoly, and Deer Detectives and show it to a ranger in the park. The program is administered by the Wisconsin Department of Natural Resources. The Wisconsin Junior Ranger program, geared to grades kindergarten through three, gives kids a chance to earn a patch and a certificate by completing the activities, much as with the Future Wisconsin Explorers.

Naturalist programs are held daily throughout the summer vacation season, with a Kiddie Walk scheduled monthly. Evening programs at the nature center (bring a chair) focus on snakes of Wisconsin, bats, and glaciers. The lectures start at 8:00 P.M., which isn't too late for youngsters. A state park sticker is required. A resident daily pass is $4.00, with a nonresident daily pass at $6.00. Resident annual passes are $15 and nonresident annual passes are $24. Before parking, motor vehicles must have an admission ticket attached to the inside of the windshield on the driver's side.

EDGERTON

The rock-ribbed town of Edgerton is the boyhood home of author Sterling North, who wrote the children's classics *So Dear to My Heart* and *Rascal*. Both books sold more than two and a half million copies and were made into Walt Disney movies. A room in the **Albion Academy Museum** (608–884–4313), at 605 Campus Lane just north of the city, is dedicated to North and his writings. The free museum is open only on Sundays from 1:00 to 4:30 P.M. throughout the year or by appointment. The academy, which was founded in 1853, is one of the oldest institutions of higher learning in Wisconsin and the first to offer co-ed schooling. The Sterling North Society (608–884–3870 or 884–9051) has just purchased the author's Edgerton home at 409 West Rollin Street and is restoring it as a museum and literary center.

Edgerton was also the Tobacco Capital of the World at the turn of the century, with a few of the original fifty-two drying warehouses still standing. Buyers from around the world used to come to town to bid on the quality product that was grown on surrounding farms. **The Tobacco City Museum** (608–884–4614) at the junction of Albion, Swift, and Fulton streets shows off farming artifacts and memorabilia from that era. The cozy little museum is open at no charge from 9:00 A.M. to noon on Tuesdays and Thursdays. Edgerton also sponsors a **Tobacco Heritage Days** (608–884–4319 or 868–7219) celebration each July. A number of farms in the area still grow tobacco, producing a variety that is used mostly as cigar wrapping. Their drying sheds are packed with the pungent leaf during the autumn harvest season. Even from the highways kids in the backseat of a car can pick out the distinctive sheds because of their building style: They have open sides or alternating slats to allow the wind to circulate and dry the leaves.

MADISON

City of 194,591 . . . students, professors, politicians, lobbyists, government workers, and a stray real person or two. This is Mad City, Wisconsin's state capital and home of the University of Wisconsin ("We're the Rose Bowl champs of 1994," everyone says upon being introduced). It is a city built on an isthmus between Lakes Mendota and Monona, where bicycling is politically correct and three-piece suits mingle easily with torn shorts and long hair on State Street, the eclectic main drag. As such, Madison is a "capitol idea," a great place to visit for a family outing.

Start with a tour at the **capitol building** itself, perched high on a hill in the center of the city. Subsequently, the edifice is hard to miss since it seems to hover several feet off the ground. Hot air from politicians does the trick, according to locals. Parking is available in nearby multilevel city garages, which are a safer bet than trying to find an opening on the crowded one-way streets closest to the capitol. The ramps offer all-day parking for only a few dollars—well worth it, because downtown Madison is easily strollable. Be warned that Madison traffic cops are merciless and have heard every "I'm from out of town" plea there has ever been. But they do smile when they hand out tickets.

Tours are held daily and on some holidays, with a tour of the governor's mansion sometimes thrown in for good measure. Free tours are offered April 1 through the end of August, on Thursdays from noon to 3:00 P.M. Call (608) 266-3554 for particulars. The marbled hallways are conducive to echoes, so tell the urchins to keep the voices down while they look for the carved stone badgers peeking out from secret recesses. Remember that it is easy to get turned around in the myriad corridors leading from the central rotunda, and dropping bread crumbs to find one's way back to the main doors (there are exits on each side) is frowned upon. If older kids are allowed to quietly tour sans parents (but still in a buddy system, of course), predetermine an assembly point and time. The main-floor information booth is a good place. Have the kids go around with a list of questions to be answered.

The child with the most correct responses can be treated to a hot fudge sundae at the university's Babcock Hall. The ice cream, made from the agricultural school's own happy Holsteins, is twelve percent butterfat instead of the standard industry ten percent. **The Babcock Hall Dairy Store** (608–262–3045) is located at 1605 Linden Drive.

Madison's Capitol Square, more commonly known as the Concourse, is the site for numerous outdoor activities, from the **Taste of Madison** (608–255–2537), with its sixty-plus restaurants, five music stages, a waiters' race, and a kiddie korner with games and activities to a celebration of **June Dairy Month** when cows—live cows—are brought to the square. As part of the program, kids can try their hand at milking. Picnics are popular while listening to the classical music concerts presented by the **Wisconsin Chamber Orchestra** the last Wednesday in June, each July Wednesday, and the first Wednesday in August. A **Farmer's Market,** opening at 6:00 A.M., is also held on the Concourse on Saturdays throughout the summer and into the autumn harvest season. Send the kids around to buy fresh beans, apples, tomatoes, and other produce. Then they can help carry the agricultural treasures back to home or hotel. The market makes for a friendly stopover for munchables while on the way through town on a vacation.

Art Fair on the Square, held the weekend after the Fourth of July, brings together thousands of strollers and gawkers interested in pieces from the traditional to "the what the heck is that" contemporary. Street performers, stilt walkers, and other entertainers flit through the crowds. The kids can watch the Peruvian musicians, the English Morris dancers, the fire eaters, the sword swallowers, and even the governor making their rounds while Mom and Dad look for the perfect painting to hang on the living room wall. The Madison Art Center (608–257–0158) can also provide details on all the fun and activity at the art show. Call the Greater Madison Convention and Visitors Bureau (800–373–6376, extension 206) for details on Dairy Month activities, as well as other events on the Square.

Madison is a town for active folks, whether ice-fishing fans or golfers. For runners the **Mad City Marathon** at the end of May brings together runners—and walkers—of all ages for an extended loop around the city. The race starts on the south side of Lake Monona, loops up to the north, through downtown and past the capitol building, around the upscale Maple Grove neighborhood where the governor lives on the shore of Lake Monona, out to the west side of town, and back past Lake Wingra. Not everyone needs to gallop the entire length, especially with kids in tow, and there are varying distances in which to participate. Many families take part as a group, with volunteers assigned to help with family reunions. Call (800) 373–6376 for the particulars.

A surprised guest may find himself or herself on the radio during the nationally syndicated ***Whad'Ya Know*** program on Wisconsin Public Radio (608–263–4141). The irreverent, hilarious host, Michael Feldman, pulls people into his goofy on-air quizzes and then sends jokes sailing out into the ether. Sitting in the back of the room doesn't hide bashful guests. Feldman often crawls over chairs to get to folks for a comment or two. Yet that is all part of the fun and a good way to win a silly prize. The program is broadcast Saturday mornings from the Parliamentary Room, in the university's Vilas Hall. Seating is at 9:00 A.M., with the show starting at 10:00 A.M. Vilas is located on University Avenue and Park Street. A massive building, with its skyway over University Avenue, it is hard to miss. The box office is located at 821 University Avenue. Admission is free but on a first-come, first-served basis.

Since the 1960s the Beverly Ski-Billies (actually, the official name is the **Capital City Ski Team**) have been entertaining audiences with their fantastic aquatic acrobatics each summer. Barefoot skiing, jumping, and many more pro techniques are part of the show, which takes place on the blue-green waters of Lake Monona. Bring a blanket, a cooler, and the kids and stake out a grassy site in Law Park for the free shows, held at 7:00 P.M. Thursdays and Sundays from May through September. Law Park snuggles up to the lake, on the corner of Blair Street and John Nolen Drive in downtown Madison. The information number for the team is (608) 873–8167.

The university is a great resource for entertainment, cultural offerings, sports, term-paper research and just hanging out. The last is especially best inside the Memorial Union or on the veranda in the back, overlooking Lake Mendota. Perching there for a time gives the kids a realistic look at what college life is all about. And it is the place to look cool. Occasionally a Hollywood movie is filmed on campus because site locators love the Ivy League (and low cost) look of the Big Red One. Classical, folk, and rock concerts are regularly held in the numerous halls, art galleries explode with color, and lectures are open to the public. Call the university athletics information number (608–262–1911) for details on sporting events. The main campus number is (608) 262–1234, and the operator can direct calls to the appropriate department hosting an event. Many of the university's offices actually open at 6:00 A.M., with hours until 5:00 P.M. The sports information office is located at 1440-A Monroe Street (608-262-1440).

Because Madison is the home of state and federal governmental offices and related service agencies, there are many other to-do opportunities for families on the run. The **U.S. Forest Service Products Laboratory,** 1 Gifford Pinchot Drive (608–231–9200), is a great place to knock on wood for good luck. All the factors of what makes wood are studied to determine how it can be used in construction, science, and other realms. Free tours are held from 2:00 to 3:00 P.M. Monday through Thursday for visitors twelve years old and above. Plenty of handout material is available for the youngster needing information for botany class or woodworking.

The city is kid-oriented, amid the bustle of grownup stuff to see and do. The **Madison Children's Museum,** 100 State Street (608–256–0158) is a hands-on, jump-right-in facility where even little wallflowers can gain the confidence to try a scientific experiment or a craft of some kind. Eye-level exhibits are aimed at kids from toddler to grade-school ages. The museum is open for herds of youngsters 10:00 A.M. to 5:00 P.M. Tuesday through Saturday and 1:00 to 5:00 P.M. Sunday. Admission is $2.00 for all ages. The **Henry Vilas Zoo,** 702 South Randall (608–266–4732) has performing elephants, fuzzy bears, prowling lions, frantic monkeys, and dozens of other creatures from jungle, desert, forest, and mountain. Friendly, well-informed curators can answer questions from even the smallest visitor, and regular kid programs are offered on weekends throughout the year. Simply call for details. The zoo is small enough to take in on an afternoon, but still large enough to have plenty of exotic and near-at-home species. Admission is free.

MERRIMAC

Cross the Wisconsin River on State Highway 113 in Merrimac via the free ferryboat, one of the few remaining such state-owned vessels in the country. Holding twelve cars, or the equivalent number of packed kids, the boat runs twenty-four hours a day, from mid-April through early December. Underwater cables pull the vessel from shore to shore, about a ten-minute ride. The **Col-Sac II** (derived from Columbia and Sauk counties, which the ferry links) is operated by the Wisconsin Department of Transportation. A small ice-cream stand, on the north shore, offers several dozen exotic flavors, including elephant's foot ice cream, filled with chocolate swirls and nuts. A restroom is on the south shore. Once you're positioned in the line of cars waiting to board, it is difficult to pull off to one side if Kid No. 1 is the bathroom when the boat is ready to load. Mom and Dad can always wave from the deck to the tardy one, who will have to catch the next run.

MOUNT HOREB

When a guest says "Pass the mustard" at the **Mount Horeb Mustard Museum** (608–437–3986), the clerks might be a little puzzled. After all, there are several thousand varieties of mustards on the shelves in this neat little store at 109 East Main Street. There are the fiery types, the bland types, the wine-based types, the down-to-earth types—stacks upon stacks of jars, bottles, bags, and boxes. Try the Inner Beauty sweet papaya mustard from Costa Rica; the Royal Bohemian Mustard, handmade by Ed "the Radish King" Pavlik of Ladysmith, Wisconsin; or the Run for Water Mustard from Mound Edgecomb, Maine. No hot dog or hamburger will ever taste the same. Samples are offered and recipes given out in profusion. Ever try mustard on ice cream? Give the kids a taste and check their reaction. It might be a surprise. The shop is open year-round during regular business hours, usually 9:00 A.M. to 5:00 P.M.

Mount Horeb was originally a Scandinavian farming community, and many touches of the Norwegian and Swedish settlers are still found. Several gift shops feature items from Oslo, Stockholm, Copenhagen, and Helsinki. The stores are easily identified, not just by the various national flags but by the trolls peeking out from almost every corner. Several large carvings of the ugly folk characters are on the street corners downtown. The **Wisconsin Folk Museum** (608–437–4742) has tons of artifacts from the good old pioneer days on display. Baskets, quilts, and woodcarvings abound. Much of the furniture in the exhibit has the intricate rosemaling style of painting adorning chair backs and dresser fronts. The free folk museum, just around the corner from the mustard musuem, is open daily May 1 through October from noon to 5:00 P.M. and on weekends until Christmas.

NORTH FREEDOM

Take a ride into the past at the **Mid-Continent Railway Museum.** While the fifty-minute runs are held four times a day throughout the summer, a ride aboard the train in the autumn or winter is the most scenic and nostalgic. Old No. 1385 pulls its string of coaches through the countryside tinged by Jack Frost in the fall and then plows through the snow when Old Man Winter does his thing. The train will stop several times for kids to hop off and scoot out to photo-snapping spots. In the winter the train backs up after unloading the shutterbugs and slips around a scenic bend. Then, with whistle blowing and steam snorting into the frozen air, the engine chugs back around the corner for a fantastic picture opportunity. The ensuing camera shutters clicking sound like crickets lost on a frozen lake. To get to the museum, take State Highway 136 west to County Road PF and then south to North Freedom. Volunteers oversee the car repair shops and present the rides, dressed as old-time engineers and conductors. Several dozen pieces of rolling stock are on the sidings, including several European train cars. Some of the museum members even have their own sleepers, where they can sprawl on holiday visits between tinkering with these giant locomotives. Call (608) 524–2123. Trains depart four times a day from mid-May to Labor Day and weekends until mid-October. The museum is open

9:30 A.M. to 5:00 P.M. A family fare (two adults and two or more children) is $18; individual prices are also charged.

PARDEEVILLE

Lareau's World of Miniature Buildings (608–429–2848), on Highway 22 south of Pardeeville, is a family place. The museum holds an intricate assortment of scale models of Mount Rushmore, the Washington Monument, the Statue of Liberty, and dozens more. All the pieces were made from bits of wood, Styrofoam, and concrete. The museum is open daily 10:00 A.M. to 5:00 P.M. from Memorial Day to late October. Admission is charged.

REEDSBURG

Junior and Muffy might not know the name Norman Rockwell, but they can surely identify with the characters in his paintings. The artist spent his life chronicling the ups and downs of ordinary folks in situations so real that they seem to leap from the pages. Subsequently, the youngsters will probably enjoy the **Museum of Norman Rockwell Art,** which showcases some 4,000 pieces of the famed illustrator's work. The collection has been called the largest of its kind in the world, with curators always interested in finding more pieces. So rummage through the attic and garage in search of a collector's treasure and bring it with you on a visit. If you find something previously unduplicated in the collection, your family has friends for life. The museum is located at 227 South Park Street (608–524–2123) in Reedsburg. The museum is open 11:00 A.M. to 4:00 P.M. Mondays through Saturdays, November to April. Summer hours are 9:30 A.M. to 5:00 P.M. Admission is $4.00; $3.00 for seniors and AAA members; and free for ages twelve and under. Guests receive a card entitling them to free admission and gift shop discounts for the entire year.

The **Pioneer Log Village and Museum** (608–524–2807), at the juncture of State Highways 23 and 33, includes a school, a store, and other buildings dating from the Civil War era. Visitors can poke around the church and blacksmith shop to get an idea of life during the so-called good old days. The complex of historic structures is open Memorial Day through September. Admission is charged.

RUDOLPH

The **Grotto Gardens and Wonder Cave,** at 6975 Grotto Avenue in Rudolph, might seem a slow place to take the kids for a visit, located as it is behind St. Philip's parish school. But maybe that's OK. The memorials there to veterans and victims of World Wars I and II are impressive, as are the gardens, with their explosive variety of well-tended annuals and perennials. But the kids will probably simply enjoy roaming the grounds, peeking into secret recesses, and exploring the cave, which can take up to a half-hour. Inside are lighted shrines to saints and other religious exhibits; the dark tunnel has plenty of spooky, jump-out-and-scare-you possibilities for those who aren't spiritually inclined at the time. While the cave and gift shop are open only from Memorial Day to Labor Day, the grounds are always open for strolling. Call (715) 435–3120. The grotto was built by Father Phillip J. Wagner and Edmund Rybicki in the 1920s. A visit there is free, but a $2.50 donation is asked when visiting the cave.

SAUK CITY

Sauk City is the launch point for canoe trips down the Lower Wisconsin River, with a number of outfitters in town who can supply everything from vessel to life jacket. They will even pick up you and the gang at a pre-designated point from a day to a week after taking off. The Saukville Chamber of Commerce (Box 238, Saukville 53080; 414–284–0438) can help with names. The Wisconsin is the state's longest and mightiest river, called the Workhorse because it was used to float logs downstream, carry freight and passengers upstream, and generate power. Camping is allowed on the numerous sandbars that peek up out of the water. Choose one that sits high out of the river, pitch a tent with extra-long pegs to prevent a sudden wakeup when the canvas collapses, or sleep under the stars. Assign one of the kids as the bug repellent carrier because mosquitoes the size of aircraft carriers like to nibble.

Natural Bridge State Park (608–356–8301, at the conjunction of Highway 12 and County C, offers fishing, hiking, and picnicking. The highlight of the 560-acre park is a sandstone arch that towers 25 feet high and 35 feet wide, the result of eroding wind, water, and ice. Prehistoric people used to live in the area.

SPRING GREEN

While Spring Green may be small (only about 2,000 resident population), it is big in things to see and do. It is a hub for central Wisconsin canoeing, camping, hiking, biking, golfing, poking around, and lolling under a maple to contemplate how to pay for college tuitions. This is the so-called driftless region of Wisconsin, where glaciers didn't rumble, so the ridges and valleys are worn by erosion, not by Ice Age action. This means there are still hills to pedal up and scoot down, rivers cut into deep limestone banks, and hiking trails across high ridges with vistas where on a clear day one can see almost forever, or at least 100 square miles.

This was at least one reason why famed architect Frank Lloyd Wright loved this area so much. He established his **Taliesin** as a "hope and a haven" for creative thinking, a complex of buildings and energy that shaped design for generations. At Taliesin he developed plans for the Imperial Hotel in Japan, the Johnson Wax administration building in Racine, and other marvelous structures. Tours of his former home, now a National Historical Landmark, are regular components of the tourist scene in the area. A visitor center (608–588–7900) and restaurant at the intersection of State Highway 23 and County Highway C is the starting point for the tours. Wright designed this elaborate, 300-foot-long building as well. Hours for 2-mile, 90-minute walking tours of the site are 9:30 A.M. to 2:30 P.M. Mondays through Saturdays ($20, adults, $10 children). From May through October, Wright's Hillside Home School offers tours on the hour 9:00 A.M. to 4:00 p.m ($8.00, adults; $4.00, five to twelve; free under five). Admission for two-hour exclusive tours of Wright's home is $40 per person; call for details.

Architects still work and learn at the Taliesin complex across the highway and down the road from the visitor center, reached by van from the latter. Tours range from about an hour to a half-day or more. Smaller young

ones, naturally, might opt for the shorter version, while older kids appreciate the lengthier version because of the depth of the visit. Regardless of
which, the program highlights Wright's philosophy that land, nature, structures, and interior design should be treated as an entity. It is a concept that
even youngsters can understand after seeing up close how Wright managed
to blend all these forms into a comfortable, user-friendly environment.

There are many opportunities for the family to hop on bikes and
explore the area around Spring Green. The 20 level miles of County
Highway C and Kennedy Road take cyclists of any age along the Wisconsin
River. On the other hand, Upper Snead and Percussion Rock roads are recommended for more serious pedalers, and their steep climbs offer reward-
ing views. For mountain biking the unpaved 9 miles of Lakeview and
Snead Creek roads are a challenge. Add another 6 miles by starting from
the Upper Wyoming Valley. Experienced bikers in the area recommend a
loop consisting of a mixture of county and state roads such as Z, ZZ, 130,
and C. That 30-mile run is probably a bit much for the under-teen set but
good heart-pumping exercise for the older gang.

Canoeing along the Wisconsin River in the Spring Green area is like
dying and going to paddler's heaven. South of Sauk City and on to the west
past the Highway 23 bridge, the riverbank is relatively unspoiled by developers. Put-in points include Sauk City, Tower Hill State Park, Peck's
Landing, and Lone Rock. There are numerous sandbars on which to rest
(Alert! Alert! Some sandbars are enjoyed by sun and nature lovers in the
buff). Once beached, canoers can fix a meal or pitch camp for an overnight.
Be careful, however, if the kids want to swim in the river. Strong currents
can quickly pull a beginner, and even a strong swimmer for that matter,
downstream. Subsequently, insist that everyone always swim with a buddy,
and tell the kids to angle toward shore without panicking if the river does
take control.

One of the most comfortable and civilized places to stay in the Spring
Green area is the **Springs Golf Club Resort** (800–822–7774 or 608–
588–7000) on Golf Course Road off County Highway C. Accommodations
are all two-room suites, which are decorated with class. There is plenty of
room space for golf bags, cross-country skis, or extra urchins. Rates begin
at $135 on weekdays. The resort offers fantastic food in both the main
restaurant and the smaller cafe. And the exercise opportunities in a fitness

center make the Springs better than the average getaway. Advisers then can help youngsters plan a good workout while the folks go out and do eighteen holes. A 30-kilometer trail system on the ridges behind the resort can be used for hiking or cross-country skiing. The Springs does it up right, with its Gourmet Nature Hike in the autumn (call to check dates), wherein regular stops on the trail could include pheasant, wine, chocolate-covered strawberries, and other temptations quite unlike the usual granola bar. Now this is a hike the family won't forget, and yes, children are invited.

Across the street from the resort, which is actually set far back from the road on its private acreage, is the **American Players Theater** (608–588–7401). The open-air stage is devoted to the classics, primarily Shakespeare, but a bit of Molière or Chekhov might be thrown in for spice during any given season. Tell Junior to bring the mosquito lotion and Muffy the sweaters or jackets. There is no controlling the bus or the weather, so be prepared for any eventuality. Guests can picnic, order a box lunch, or even grill out. The theater wants to make everyone feel at home, so it often stages special events, including "skip out of work early" productions. A shuttle service runs from the Springs resort, so a guest doesn't need to walk the 1 mile or so from door to door. The theater season begins in June and continues through early October. Ticket prices begin at $16.50.

South of Spring Green on State Highway 23, the **House on the Rock** boggles the mind. Designed and built by artist Alex Jordan atop a 60-foot chimney of rock in the early 1940s, the house overlooks Wyoming Valley. That's a 450-foot drop, folks. Greatly expanded into a warren of museum space and living areas, the house, outbuildings, and gardens cover more than 200 acres. The kids will know something special is in the works when entering the long drive to the structure. Large urns overflowing with flowers—and dragons, elves, and imps—stand sentinel along the highway and on the road leading to the house itself. Plan to spend at least a half-day exploring all the recesses and secret places within the house. Each turn offers something excitingly different and almost overpowering, because of the amount of stuff to be found here. Everything about the House on the Rock has to do with BIG numbers, starting with the outside. Jordan and his gardeners planted 50,000 trees on his grounds and 100,000 flowers in his rock garden. The latter are augmented by 3,000 flowerpots, each with its own brilliant display.

For example, the Infinity Room has 3,246 windows and extends out over the valley floor some 218 feet. The room narrows at the end, and mirrors give the impression that it continues forever. The Heritage of the Sea Building is home to a 200-foot-long whale fighting with an octopus. The whale is longer than the Statue of Liberty is tall. More than 200 ship models line the ramps that encircle the watery battle in the three-story structure. Off to one side is a diorama of the Battle of Trafalgar, one of the most famous in English naval history.

The house also features the world's largest carousel, one that has more than 20,000 lights and 269 handmade animals (not one horse) twirling and whirling to bombastic organ accompaniment. The carousel stands 35 feet high, is 80 feet wide, and weighs 35 tons. The best time to show the masterpiece to the kids is at the end of the day, when most of the crowds have gone home. Visitors step into the enormous room from a darkened hallway and are greeted by an explosion of light and sound as the carousel begins moving. Hanging overhead are several hundred mannequins outfitted as angels in various stages of disarray. The effect on a youngster, or any old-timer with a youngster's imagination, is mouth-dropping.

The exhibits go on and on and on. Be prepared for walking a lot—up and down ramps, on spiral staircases, underneath waterfalls, and over bridges. Simply follow the arrows and no one will get lost, not even in the Hannibal Crossing the Alps diorama or amid the eighty-piece mechanical orchestra in the Circus Room or in the Organ Building, with its 45-foot-high perpetual motion clock. There are, however, strategically placed restrooms and cafeterias.

Highlights of the house? Votes go to the two-level doll merry-go-round with its several hundred bisque dolls. This is a fantastic exhibit but rather disconcerting, with all those eyes staring back at the viewer. Then there is a weapons exhibit that includes a derringer pistol concealed in a woman's wooden leg. Or how about the 250 dollhouses, furnished down to the interior lighting and wallpapering?

For the holiday season, which extends from mid-November through early January, the house displays some 6,000 Santa Claus figures, plus a collection of life-size Father Christmas characters.

Of any attraction in central Wisconsin, the House on the Rock is a must-see. No matter the age. Stupendous, simply put. Admission rates are

Perched high above the Wyoming Valley, The House on the Rock contains marvel after marvel showcased in numerous exhibits. (Courtesy The House on the Rock)

$13.50 for ages thirteen and above, $8.50 for guests seven to twelve, and $3.50 for ages four to six. Youngsters under three are free. Group rates are also available. The museum is open daily 9:00 A.M. late March through October and 10:00 A.M. in winter months. The last ticket is sold at 4:00 P.M. The museum is closed Thanksgiving, Christmas Eve Day, and Christmas Day. Call (608) 935–3639 for all the details.

STEVENS POINT

The Green Circle, a 24-mile nature trail around Stevens Point, is a fine way to see the wild side of the city . . . wild in the sense that it brings nature home to the urban folk. The Stevens Point Convention and Visitors Bureau, 23 Park Ridge Drive, (715) 344–2556, can provide maps. Hikers can also secure a free map of the trail system at the **Schmeeckle Reserve** nature center (715–346–4992) on North Point Drive. The reserve itself is part of the trail system, with woodchips and boardwalks making for easy trekking. The center is the home of the Wisconsin Conservation Hall of Fame, where noted state residents are honored for their work in preserving the environment. Numerous natural history programs are offered at the reserve, with many geared to youngsters. There is no admission charge.

The **Pacelli Panacea,** a fund-raising drive for Pacelli High School, is held annually early in September with a polka mass, a carnival, an arts and crafts show, and loads of food. The school cooks spend weeks preparing for a roast chicken feast, with parents and community residents donating baked goods for a massive sale geared to the sweet-tooth set. This is a true family festival in the good, old-time sense of the term. Guests are welcome to enter into the festivities. Call the high school (715–341–2442) for the dates. The school is located at 1301 Maria Drive, on the city's north side.

On the college level the University of Wisconsin at Stevens Point celebrates each year with its **Spud Bowl** football game, battling top-ranked teams from around the Midwest. Held at various times in the early autumn, due to a particular year's scheduling, the game is preceded by a parade, a massive cookout, games, and music. Since Stevens Point is in the heart of Wisconsin's potato-growing country, there are always plenty of spuds (hence the game name) in all varieties, from baked to French-fried. Kids watch in amazement as the elder college crowd goes through its Spud Olympics. Diving for bubble gum in bowls of mashed potatoes, potato sack races, and similar goofball events bring the community together for a laugh. Call the convention and visitors bureau at the number above for times, places, and costs for the Spud Olympics.

For a refreshing stop after a full day of trekking about town, drop by the **Stevens Point Brewery,** at the corner of Beer and Water streets. Brewers of the fabled Point Beer, the brewery also makes Spud Beer under license to the Stevens Point Chamber of Commerce during Spud Bowl time. The smooth and mellow Spud suds are made from potatoes, a staple of local agriculture scene. Tours are given throughout the day, during regular business hours. Call (715) 344–9310. The brewery also has funky, fun sweatshirts and other premiums that can be ordered by mail (call 800–369–4911).

WISCONSIN DELLS/LAKE DELTON

The Dells almost deserve a chapter unto themselves. For years Steve and the rest of the gang have visited this central Wisconsin community, a jack-in-the-box that has all the trappings of one gigantic, never-ending amusement park. There is enough here for everyone in the family, from thrill shows to balloon rallies to waterslides. Historically, the Native Americans appreciated the natural wonderslide of rock and forest for centuries before the first French sallied down the Wisconsin River to "discover" the region. The Europeans used the word *dalles,* meaning "gorge," to describe the deep canyons and hidden valleys that ranged along the shore. From that term the "dells" evolved. Since the Civil War vacationers have found the peace and quiet of the region to their liking. Over the years, however, more and more attractions were built to accommodate the growing number of guests. Subsequently, today's Dells are certainly not as remote as when the Winnebago lived here, but a cruise on the *Red Cloud* or any of the other excursion boats on the upper or lower river takes guests away from the landbound rush and glitz.

Today U.S. Highway 12/State Highway 23 is a carnival midway linking the neighboring towns of Wisconsin Dells and Lake Delton. The communities are five minutes maximum off I–90/94, with billboards in Illinois, Iowa, and Minnesota telling motorists how to get there. The Wisconsin Dells Visitor and Convention Bureau, 701 Superior Street, Wisconsin Dells 53965–0390 (800–22–DELLS or 608–254–4636), can provide tons of flyers, maps, guides, and tips on what to see and do. It offers a free annual 138-page *Travel & Attraction Guide* that tells about all the activities in the Dells area, including hours of operation, contact numbers, and related information. A large fold-out map indicates locations of all the listed sites, most of which are along U.S. Highway 12/Wisconsin Highway 23 in Lake Delton and along Wisconsin Highway 13 through downtown Wisconsin Dells. The locals have nicknamed these roadways "The Strip."

Since this is a tourist town to the *nth* degree from Memorial Day through Labor Day, the peak summer months, each attraction opens by 8:00

or 9:00 A.M. and keeps going until long after dark. Various passes, coupons, and other deals are offered, but all attractions throughout the Dells are less than $10, ensuring a cost-effective vacation that won't strain a pocketbook.

The authentic Dells is actually a more natural strip of some 15 miles of protected river frontage, with sandstone cliffs and landings at such exotic locales as Witches Gulch and Stand Rock, where visitors can hike. Tours operate from April through October. Kiosks strategically placed throughout the Dells area sell tickets for trips on the **Riverview Boat Line** (608–254–8336), the **Dells Boat Company** (608–253–1561), and the **Olson Boat Company** (608–254–8500). There is hardly anything better to do than to sit back on a deck chair, put one's feet high on a railing, lean back, and enjoy the sunshine.

For a more challenging, bouncy way to capture the spirit of the waterway, the ***Original Wisconsin Ducks*** (608–254–8751) present an hour-long, 8-mile tour on the river, Dell Creek, and Lake Delton. The Ducks are refurbished World War II amphibious landing craft, once used to race troops up on a beach during an attack. The more peaceful pursuits these days are almost as exciting. Boarding is at 1890 Wisconsin Dells Parkway (Highway 12).

Four miles of the trip ramble through Hop-along Hill and Red Bird Gorge, among other aptly named landmarks, plunging in and out of the water, careening along slopes, and defying death at every sharp turn. At least that's what it seems like, so hang on tight and enjoy the ride. And be prepared for an occasional dampening. Once back on land guests can stagger off to a fudge shop or souvenir stand to load up on goodies for the ride home. Actually, the rides are not dangerous at all, but kids love the funny patter of the drivers and the apparent edge of danger.

For real thrills **Tommy Bartlett's Ski, Sky, and Stage Show** (800–254–2525) has jugglers twirling flaming batons and spinning cutlasses, contortionists who can tie themselves into double knots (and free themselves), speeding stunt boats that top 100 miles per hour as they perform tail stands and ramp jumps, skyflier daredevils dangling from hovering helicopters, and, of course, the ski show itself. Three performances are held daily, rain or shine, with a regular 8:30 P.M. laser explosion to top off an evening of lovely young ladies and hunky guys doing amazing things on water skis.

Impresario Tommy Bartlett, who looks like a beaming Santa Claus, with his white bead and jovial grin, has been at this for what seems to be centuries. His promotional bumper stickers have appeared around the world in the oddest places. Always thinking of new ways to entertain guests, Bartlett also devised the **Robot World & Exploratory** (608–254–2525). The computerized touch-screen games, gravity experiments, and robotic house are guaranteed to grab attention. Hair literally stands on end during some of the electrical energy experiments, much to the delight of the kids.

The list of Dells attractions is seemingly endless. One important stop is the **Stand Rock Indian Ceremonial** (608–253–7444), which begins at 8:45 P.M. By car the site is 4 miles north of Wisconsin Dells on Stand Rock Road. If you're going by boat, the trip is launched at 7:45 P.M. from the Upper Dells landing. Native American dancers from several tribes put on demonstrations nightly and talk with visitors about the meaning of the movements. Kids are especially welcome to ask questions. For another Native American touch, the **Winnebago Indian Museum** (608–254–2268) showcases the heritage of this major Wisconsin tribe, with artifacts, photos, and memorabilia. The museum is 2 miles north of Wisconsin Dells on a spur road just off State Highways 12 and 16. Look for the signs.

Even with the dozens of motels and hotels, most of which have waterfalls, swimming pools, play areas, and other amenities, outdoor camping is still popular. **Rocky Arbor State Park** (608–254–8001) and **Mirror Lake State Park** (608–254–2333) are two prime locales far enough away from the neon and wax museums to offer that all-important solitude (in February the state park's cross-country ski trails are lighted by thousands of candles for nighttime ambience). Private campgrounds include **Spring Brook** (800–254–2267 or 608–254–4343), **Sherwood Forest** (608–254–7080), **Tepee Park** (608–253–3122), **Holiday Shores** (608–254–2727), and numerous others. It is always a good idea to ask about on-site facilities, location, and amenities because some camping areas are resort-oriented and others offer a more primitive style of outdoor adventure. The Dells convention bureau can provide listings. Don't worry about being too far away from civilization because **Pizza Pub** (414–254–7877) will deliver shrimp fettuccine, chicken cacciatore, Italian sandwiches, and pizza (yes, with anchovies if requested) to your campsite. The pub has a kids' menu with mouse-size portions. Just ask. Don't worry about dripping sauce. You're camping.

The Dells area resorts are in a geographic league by themselves. Don't be confused to find an **Aloha Beach** (608–253–4741) or the **Caribbean Club Resort** (800–800–6981), much less the **Copa Cabana** (800–364–COPA), the **Monte Carlo** (608–254–8761), and the **Polynesian** (800–27–ALOHA). Regardless of the names, this is still the delightful Dells.

After a long day of exploring, wiping spilled malts off the rear seat, driving, and more driving, it is natural that Mom and Dad can't stand up straight. This is true especially when visiting the **Wonder Spot** (608–254–4224), where "you have to see it to believe it." This is one of these puzzling places where everything is off-kilter and kids seem to roll uphill. The building, where even sitting down is a challenge, is a real photographer's holiday. The Wonder Spot is on U.S. Highway 12 near the bridge. For another amazing look-see, visit **Ripley's Believe It or Not Museum** (608–253–7556) in downtown Wisconsin Dells. Based on the old syndicated newspaper column, the museum has plenty of the unusual and odd for kids to laugh at or groan about.

On a more recognizable level, little kids will enjoy **Wisconsin Deer Park** (608–253–2041), a 28-acre wildlife exhibit set back in the forest away from U.S. Highway 12. Some of the deer can be petted, while the big bucks are best viewed from afar.

While the naturalness of the Wisconsin River is OK, as far as water adventure goes in the mind of a kid, youngsters really go for the slides and bumper cars at all the Dells water parks. Some fifty different splash-type activities are in **Noah's Ark** (608–254–6351), where the waterlogged gang from the backseat can spend days getting wrinkled and pink. Noah's Ark calls itself the largest such theme park in the United States, a claim that is certainly hard to dispute. Bermuda Triangle, Thunder Rapids, Kowabunga, the Wave, Slidewinders (one of twenty-seven slides) . . . the list goes on and on. Twelve restaurants are on the grounds, in case the hungers hit between dives down the Chute Shooters. All-day passes are honored until 8:00 P.M.

Riverview Park & Waterworld (608–254–2608), located near the boat docks on Highway 12, adds even more whoop and holler to a hot summer afternoon. Picnic pavilions and free observation areas (for the non-waterlogged) are available at the Wave Pool and elsewhere on the grounds. The Giant Log Walk and Kiddie Tube Run are the most fun, but the Oceans of Waves pool runs right up there on the heart-in-the-mouth scale as well. A kids' ticket allows all-day unlimited use of the pools, go-cart tracks, petting zoo, bumper boats, innertube rides, funhouse, and other activities.

The Tidal Wave at **Family Land** (608–254–7766) is another rip-roaring surfing adventure, almost as good as the Australian coast, where the waves of summer crash against the shore. The Double Tubes, Blue Magnum, Fountain of Youth, Raging River, Demon Drop, and Double Rampage also ensure a vacation without need of a bathtub. What better way to keep a kid clean? Well, you could also try a scrubdown aboard the Timber Mountain log flume ride at Timber Falls (608–254–8414), near the Wisconsin River Bridge and Stand Rock Road. A bunch of folks can get wet together as their log ride plunges into a pool with the appropriate drenching.

Several other attractions combine water with minigolf (**Shipwreck Lagoon,** 608–253–7772, and **Pirate's Cove,** 608–254–8336), fishing (**Beaver Springs Fishing Park,** 608–253–7100), and ski boats, parasailing, paddleboats, and canoes (**Lake Delton Water Sports,** 608–254–8702). Obviously, the Wisconsin Dells area has a thing about H_2O.

For more landlocked adventure (around a reflecting pool, of course) bring the little ones over to **Storybook Gardens** (608–253–2391), where costumed fairy tale characters wander the grounds. A fairy princess has a magic wand with which to bestow wishes and Little Bo-Peep is always looking for her sheep. Youngsters are invited to participate in a daily parade around the site at 12:30 P.M. from mid-June through the end of August. Musical instruments, flags, and signs are provided.

With all that activity a family should be as hungry as a lumberjack. **Paul Bunyan Meals** (608–254–8717) on the Highway 13 exit off I–90/94 has been a staple eatery in the Dells for generations. Featuring an all-you-can-eat chicken and fish fry on Friday, along with spaghetti and potato pancakes, the restaurant looks like a cook shanty in the woods. Long wooden benches, checked tablecloths, and logging artifacts make for a

North Woods ambience. Parents will appreciate the huge pots of coffee placed on every table, as well as the special kids' prices.

Downhill skiing is an option at **Cascade Mountain** (608–742–5588) from late November through March and at the **Skyline Ski Area** (608–339–3421) from early December through March 11. **Christmas Mountain Village** (608–254–3972) also has downhill and cross-country packages, ski lessons for kids, and sleigh rides. Christmas Mountain also sponsors a Winter Carnival in February, with a chili cook-off, live music, and dogsled races. Get the details from the Dells chamber of commerce, which can send a package outlining all the winter family activities and events.

WISCONSIN RAPIDS

The finals of the **Little Britches Rodeo** are held at the beginning of September each year at the Lazy B Ranch, 5511 Eightieth Street South, in Kellner, a Wisconsin Rapids rural suburb. Age-groups between six and eleven, eleven and fifteen, and fifteen through high school compete in bull riding, saddle and bareback bronco riding, goat tying, calf roping, team roping, pole bending, and barrel racing. For a weekend of jumping, flopping, flipping, ya-hooing, and hanging on tight, the rodeo can't be beat. The entrants are serious about their riding and roping, and many move on to college teams, with some eventually turning pro. The bulls and horses are big, really big, so there is nothing childish about the competition; however, a sheep-riding contest for little kids is always a funny sight, with the tots trying to mount the mutton and ride off into the sunset. Events are held simultaneously in two large arenas, so viewers sometimes have to move from bleacher seat to bleacher seat in order to catch action on the other side. Several thousand people, mostly families, turn out to yell encouragement and help dust off the jeans after a tumble. Tell the youngsters to watch the rear end of horses and to watch where they step if they go out for a stroll. A small admission fee is charged. Call the Wisconsin Rapids Chamber of Commerce (715–423–1830) for details. Put the kids in cowboy hats, boots, and jeans, and away they go. Vendors on-site can outfit even the tiniest cowpoke.

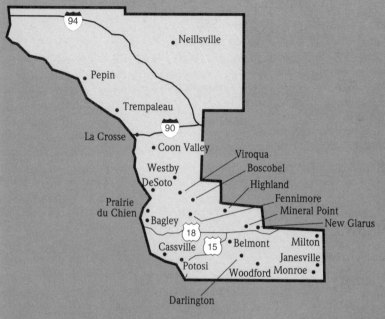

Neillsville

Pepin

Trempaleau

94

90

La Crosse

Coon Valley

Viroqua

Westby

Boscobel

DeSoto

Highland

Prairie
du Chien

Fennimore

Bagley

Mineral Point

18

New Glarus

Cassville

15

Belmont

Milton

Potosi

Janesville

Woodford

Monroe

Darlington

South-Southwest

SOUTH-SOUTHWEST

atfish, historical homes, family history, buckskinners, eagles, doll museums—name the words and there will be something akin to what you want on a getaway. No matter if the backseat gang is two or twenty, southwestern Wisconsin has an adventure for them.

Ogle an old-fashioned steam locomotive, count turtle shells outside a commercial fisherman's shed, try a hand at golf, walk the same ground as French explorers did 300 years ago. This is the place for pulling together history and contemporary fun. This is also a reflective part of the state, with tales of Native Americans massacred because they loved their land and of Army grunts in Vietnam who loved and died for similar causes. Memorials to both can be found here, tucked into fog-shrouded corners where tears and unfulfilled dreams mingle. Take the kids to these sites and stand quietly. Let the spirit enter their hearts. And then move on to more discoveries.

This is a landscape steeped in secret histories, made up of lead miners, of farmers, of immigrants, of plain people looking for new lives. The fertile soil and the rich waterways shaped every settler's outlook on life—upbeat, vibrant, and ready for action. That has resulted in a destination tailor-made for a great vacation.

BAGLEY

Take Grant Country Highway VV along the Mississippi to **Wyalusing State Park** (608–996–2261) in Bagley for its camping facilities, hiking trails, and picnic sites. Indian mounds dating back 1,000 years can be found on the bluff overlooking the river, on the Sentinel Ridge Walk. On one marked overlook show the youngsters where the Mississippi and Wisconsin rivers converge. The park, sprawling over 2,700 acres, is a veritable wildlife resort. Whitetail deer, bald eagles, Canada geese, wild turkeys, turkey vultures, muskrats, possums, and raccoons can sometimes be spotted.

In the winter Wyalusing has excellent groomed and tracked cross-county ski trails, making it ideal for all classes of skiers. Since the terrain ranges from flat to hilly, from wooded to open, the variety keeps up the interest of even the littlest skier. Toilets and water are on-site. The park is open 6:00 A.M. to 11:00 P.M. A state park sticker is required. A resident daily pass is $4.00, with a nonresident daily pass at $6.00. Resident annual passes are $15, and nonresident annual passes are $24. Before parking motor vehicles must have an admission ticket attached to the inside of the windshield on the driver's side.

BELMONT

Trek to the top of the observation tower atop the **Belmont Mound,** nearly 400 feet above the city. It is located 2 miles north of Belmont from Highway 151, off County Highway G. From the 64-foot-high tower, visitors can see three states. The name Belmont, in fact, comes from the French phrase *belle mont,* meaning "beautiful mountain." The mound is covered with oaks and walnut trees, with raspberry and blackberry bushes. Morel mushroom hunters love poking around in the forest for these special treats. The year-round park is maintained by the Belmont Lions Club.

Take the kids on a walking expedition to see the Devil's Dining Table, a flat rock about 40 feet across perched on a pedestal of stone. A few feet away is the Devil's Chair, an appropriately shaped chair. Also nearby is the Cave, a dark passageway through a giant rock and a perfect site for scrambling youngsters.

Belmont, tucked into a corner of the intersection of U.S. Highway 151, Wisconsin Highway 126, and Lafayette County Highway C, was

Wisconsin's first capital. A state park in the city preserves the Wisconsin Territorial Hall and the Supreme Court Building. Both buildings date from the 1830s and can be toured. There is no admission for the tours, which run during summer months between 9:00 A.M. and 4:30 P.M.

After checking out the hall and courtroom, take a hike . . . on the **Pecatonica Trail,** which follows a Milwaukee Road rail line for almost 10 miles between Belmont and Calamine. Look for the trail signs in either town. The trail begins in Calamine on County Road G and ends in Platteville on Wisconsin Highway 151. When completed by the turn of the century, the trail will be 17 miles long. The gravel-and-cinder-surfaced trail travels along the Bonner Branch of the Pecatonica River. Walkers and bikers are welcome in the nonwinter months. When the snow flies, snowmobilers and cross-country skiers can utilize the pathway. Bonner Branch is a swift-moving little creek that swings back and forth under the trail, making it necessary to have twenty-four bridges on the stretch between the two towns. That totals 1,306 feet of planking. The trail corridor is perfect for spotting quail, pheasant, squirrels, woodchucks and occasionally deer.

BOSCOBEL

Several farms in the area have shops featuring homemade crafts or foods, and some are occasionally open for home visits and overnights. To secure a map and other information, contact Farm Trails in Southwest Wisconsin, 4478 Riley Road, Boscobel 53805 (608–375–5798). Near Boscobel, in the hamlet of Blue River—reached by following State Highway 133 northeast to Eagle Cave Road—is **Eagle Cave Natural Park** (608–537–2988). This is the state's largest onyx cave, where guided tours are presented during summer vacation months. The brave and hardy can even camp there during the winter. Bats? Not many! Admission is charged.

CASSVILLE

Stonefield Village (608–725–5210), a state historical society property on Grant County Highway W, about 8 miles south of Prairie du Chien, is a reproduction of an 1890s village. Craftworkers and interpreters show guests around the village. Buildings include a railroad depot, shops, a firehouse, homes, and a school. The best time to visit is an early summer morning when the Mississippi River fog still hugs the maples and oaks, when it seems as if all life has paused for a fraction of a second, but just enough to bring another era into today. The village is open 9:00 A.M. to 5:00 P.M. daily, Memorial Day weekend through Labor Day. Ticket sales end one hour before closing.

This region is called Wisconsin's Hidden Valleys Country because of the secrets and hideaways found along the backcountry roads. The name is apt because all sorts of magic can occur here. In mid-June Stonefield Children's Days present a hands-on adventure for kids by showing them how to process honey, cook on a wood-fired stove, and bake bread from scratch.

Across County Highway V V is **Nelson Dewey State Park** (608–725–5210), named after the state's first governor. Camping is available in the park, where a predawn visitor to a tent site might be a fox, skunk, or raccoon. Be sure to get the family out along the trail through the park's ten-acre prairie, with its hundreds of varieties of plants, ranging from the bluish pasqueflower to June grass. The prairie grows in height as the season advances through the summer, with spring plants only about 1 foot tall and summer/fall plants reaching from 5 to 7 feet. Remember not to pick any of the flowers in the prairie. As the motto goes, be sure the kids take only photographs and leave only footprints.

The Nelson Dewey House, originally the former governor's home, is open 9:00 A.M. to 5:00 P.M. Friday through Sunday, on national holidays, and by special appointment.

Five other original farm buildings from the Dewey homestead can also be explored, as can several ancient Indian mounds. One group of twenty mounds is spread along the ridgetop at the highest point in the park. A smaller group of five is found south of Dewey Creek. Archaeologists estimate that they date from the late Woodland period between A.D. 600 and 1300. Remains of one of their encampments has been found near Stonefield Village. As with the flora and fauna in the park, visitors are asked to treat the mounds with respect and refrain from disturbing them. They are actually sacred to the many tribes that still reside in Wisconsin.

Take the **Cassville car ferry** (608–725–5180) across the river into Iowa. For a small fee the little boat puddles back and forth across the

Mississippi, keeping up a tradition that dates back several generations. It beats crossing via the modern highway bridges to the north in Prairie du Chien or to the south at Dubuque. The boat links Wisconsin Highways 133/81 with Iowa's Highway 52 at Millville (just south of Guttenberg). The ferry, which holds six to eight cars and trucks, operates 9:00 A.M. to 9:00 P.M. from the first weekend in May, making trips on Friday, Saturday, and Sunday until Memorial Day. During the summer vacation season, it runs seven days a week until Labor Day and then weekends again until October 31. The last trip from Cassville departs at 8:20 P.M., and the last trip from Iowa departs at 8:40 P.M.

COON VALLEY

In Coon Valley you'll find **Norskedalen** (meaning "Norwegian Valley"), the home of the University of Wisconsin–La Crosse Foundation's 400-acre arboretum. Maple-dappled hills, rushing trout streams (the city calls itself the Trout Capital of the Midwest), native plantings, and sculpture make up the grounds, with trails open year-round for seasonal hiking and cross-country skiing. Norskedalen (608–452–3424) is located on Vernon County Highway PL, just off County Highway P. It is open year-round, from 9:00 A.M. to 4:30 P.M. Mondays through Saturdays. Hours on Sundays are noon to 4:30 P.M. Admission is $3.00 per person; $2.00 for children; family admission is $10.00.

Bekkum Homestead, a pioneer farm on the Norskedalen grounds, brings back memories of early Scandinavian settlers and is also open for touring, except in winter. The Thrune Visitor Center there is open 9:00 A.M. to 4:30 P.M. Monday through Saturday and noon to 4:30 P.M. Sunday. Classes and programs on Scandinavian heritage are regularly held.

Coon Valley sponsors an Old-Fashioned Threshing Bee each September, at which kids can watch the huffing, puffing ancient steam threshers; eat a farmer's picnic outside; and see how grain was harvested one hundred years ago. The event is held at the Bekkum Homestead. For Halloween there is the Ghoulees in the Goulees Haunted Hike, going through some of the darkest country this side of Count Dracula's estate. The hike can be preeetttty scary, so kids have to take care of moms and dads like us who tend to be frightened at all sorts of silly stuff like this. For

Norskedalen's Bekkum Homestead, a pioneer farm, contains a corncrib, granary, chicken coop, barn, and much more. (Courtesy Bekkum Homestead)

information, call the visitor center at Norskedalen. Admission is the same as for a regular visit to the historic site.

DARLINGTON

The Darlington Fire Department sponsors annual **canoe races** each June along the winding Pecatonica River, starting at the Calamine Bridge on Lafayette County Trunk G. A $10 entry fee per canoe is payable to the Darlington Fire Department. The finish line is 1 block past the City Bridge in Darlington itself. Two trophies are awarded to the canoe that finishes first in each division, with medallions given to second- and third-place finishes. This can be a total family affair, with classes for girls seventeen and under, high school boys, boys in grade school, mixed men and women teams, women paddlers, parent and children teams (kids need to be thirteen and under), men's teams, Cub Scout and parents, Boy Scouts, and racing canoes.

Due to the width of the river, canoes are launched in groups of up to three at a time, at two- to three-minute intervals. Starting times are then radioed to the finish line, with winners declared on a comparative time basis.

During the weekend of the official canoe sprints, the community also has inner tube races on the river, softball tournaments, pony rides, coed volleyball, 5- and 2-mile runs (plus a kids' 1-mile run), talent shows, an arts and crafts fair, Native American dancers, fireworks, a princess pageant, and many other family-oriented events. For information contact the fire department organizers at (608) 776–3773 or the University of Wisconsin Extension Office–Lafayette County branch in the Agricultural Building, 627 Washington Street, Darlington 53530 (608–776–4820).

A **dairy breakfast** on a nearby farm is also part of the fun. All the neighbors get together at a friend's home for omelettes, cheese, sundaes, applesauce, ham, muffins, and lots of milk and coffee. Of course, everyone is invited for the great food, the conversation, and a chance to check out the cows. The breakfast is held rain or shine, usually from 6:30 to 10:30 A.M., when everyone rushes back to town to get ready for one of the canoe race events. The Extension Office will have details, whether the breakfast will be at the Ed and Kerry Grazt Farm again, over on Golf Course Road, or at another farm. Breakfasts generally cost $3.00 for adults, with kids under age twelve $2.00. Preschoolers are free.

All-terrain vehicle (ATV) riders can also take advantage of the 51²/₅ miles of rough and rugged marked trails in the Darlington area. But be sure all riders have helmets and that no one exceeds the 30 miles per hour speed limit. For an idea of the terrain, consider that one link whoops over Roller Coast Road just south of the city.

Since Darlington is located in the heart of dairy country as well, the system has linked with other communities, such as Monroe, Browntown, South Wayne Gratiot, and Mineral Point, in forming the **Cheese Country Recreational Trail**. The trail system accommodates horseback riders, hikers, snowmobilers, bikers, all-terrain vehicles, and skiers. There are at least thirty cheese factories in the three counties making up the trail system: Green, Lafayette, and Iowa counties. Some sections of the Cheese Country Trail have incorporated elements of the Pecatonica Trail. Links are marked for the appropriate use—for instance, ATVs aren't allowed where horses can be ridden. So be alert for signage. A $6.00 trail user fee is required and is available for purchase at most gas stations near the trail and at other businesses. Call the UW Extension Office in Darlington, (608) 776–4820, for details.

Darlington is also the seat of Lafayette County and has sponsored a museum at its old depot building, with exhibits outlining the history of the railroads in the vicinity and their impact on the town. The building is located in the 300 block of Washington Street, 1 block west of Main Street. Operated by the Lafayette County Historical Society, it is open daily in June, July, and August, usually from 9:00 A.M. to 5:00 P.M. The museum is free. Call the UW Extension Office, at the number given above.

DESOTO

The hamlet of DeSoto, lying along the Mississippi River, hosts a three-day **Fly-Fishing Tournament** in mid-August, featuring a kids' fishing contest that lets the youngsters show the old-timers how to bring in the Big Ones. There are also a carnival, a chicken barbecue, a steak dinner, and parades. Call (608) 648–2137 for all the latest information, plus signup details for young anglers.

DeSoto, located on the Bad Axe River, which flows into the Mississippi, was the site of a massacre during the Black Hawk War in the 1830s. Several hundred Sac and Fox women, children, and warriors were killed there as they tried to flee American troops on the Wisconsin side. Many who escaped the gunfire of the soldiers drowned in the fast-flowing river. Others were killed when they reached the Iowa banks, where their traditional enemies, the Sioux, were waiting for them with hatchets and knives. A historical marker is located on Wisconsin Highway 35, the Great River Road, near DeSoto, a cluster of homes stretched along the highway.

FENNIMORE

The **Fennimore Doll Museum,** located at 1140 Lincoln Avenue (608–922–4100), attracts kids of all ages. Even guys can get a kick out of the Star Wars and action figure characters on display. More than 5,000 dolls of varying eras peer out from their glass display cases, including some ancient dolls discovered in Mexico. Most of the toys have smiles, though some are serious. They are made of wood, glass, stone, pewter, precious metals, and plain plastic. A local farm woman began collecting the dolls some twenty years ago and decided to donate them to her hometown, to give something the kids in the small rural town could enjoy without having to travel for hours to some big-city museum. Even if a visitor isn't that interested in the entire collection, the magnitude of the 1,000-figure Barbie display is awesome. Almost every representative Barbie is there, from the very first to all the buxom bombshell's friends from over the years. They are displayed along with their toy cars, houses, tea sets, medical bags, shoes, capes, jet skis, glitter, and consumer gloss. The museum is open daily during the summer. A small admission is charged.

HIGHLAND

While driving west on State Highway 80, pause at Highland for gas and a kid/pet pit stop, then take County Q west again to the **Spurgeon Vineyards and Winery** (608–929–7692) on Pine Tree Road. Beginning to grow grapes in 1977, the winery was finally able to make wine from its own crop in 1983. Award-winning reds and whites are now available, as are winery tours and free tastings. Mom and Dad could even give the kids a teeny sample sip if feeling very European. Pull over the car, hop out for a look, and then purchase several bottles to take home. Guests can drop by anytime.

JANESVILLE

Janesville is a city best visited by bicycle and on foot. In fact, a major section of the **Ice Age Trail** meanders along the Rock River in the city, making a biking/hiking visit part of the fun. The trail will eventually be a 1,000-mile course from northern to southern Wisconsin, tracing the outline of the last glaciers to steamroll the state. Pick up the trail at the north end of town at Riverside Golf Course on U.S. Highway 14, then follow the signage along the river, through downtown Janesville, past many of the city's architectural sights, and around to **Rotary Gardens Park** (608–752–3885) on the south side for a roll past the sculpture and landscaping. On the way pause for hot dogs, ice cream, water shows, tours of historic buildings, and chats with locals. Stop at **Kiwanis Pond,** a former gravel pit just to the northeast of Rotary Gardens, but bring plenty of worms and tackle. The pit has been transformed into a fishing hole for kids and is well stocked with bass and other denizens of the watery deep.

The family will especially love the **Rock Aqua Jays** water-ski team (800–48–PARKS). The squad of muscular guys and shapely girls gives performances at 7:00 P.M. on Wednesdays and Sundays from June through Labor Day. Bleachers are available overlooking the river in Traxler Park. **Camden Playground,** located in Palmer Park on the city's south side, is the first fully accessible park for kids who are physically and mentally challenged. The playground has a castle where stage shows are presented in the summer, plus swings, slides, and a games area. Volunteers keep the facility in tip-top shape.

But if the gang would rather run than walk, enter the **Janesville Family YMCA Half Marathon** (608–754–6654), The event, held for more than twenty years, includes a 10K road race, a 2-mile run/walk, and a ½-mile run/walk for kids. Awards are given for the first through sixth places in each event, and all kids entering the race receive some sort of prize. Following the race are a magic show and a comedy act, along with a fire truck demonstration wherein the little ones can climb on the rescue vehicles and talk with firefighters. McGruff, the Take-a-Bite-out-of-Crime dog, usually makes an appearance as well, to good-naturedly warn the kids to stay on the straight and narrow.

Generally, kids wouldn't be much interested in the **Lincoln–Tallman Restorations,** 440 North Jackson Street (608–752–4519), although the rambling brick home was once the home of a major Janesville businessman and friend of Abraham Lincoln. The former president actually did sleep there several times, honest. "So what?" probably indicates youngsters who might have seen one too many old mansions. But . . . wait until Halloween, when creepy (albeit friendly) things crawl about. During the haunting season the house is decorated with plenty of spooky this-'n'-thats. In fact, a full-blown Victorian funeral is presented in the parlor. One year the place hosted a production of **Murder & Mayhem** in Rock County, wherein performers told true stories of area crimes, in appropriately darkened rooms. And maybe Lincoln returns for a chatty visit. Kids will have to come with their parents just to be sure. Here are some extra details on the Tallman place for the trivia file and school reports: The home was one of the first in the country to have indoor plumbing and central heating.

The complex is open for tours 11:00 A.M. to 4:00 P.M. Saturdays and Sundays from February through May and in October and Tuesdays through Sundays from June through September. It is also open Thanksgiving weekend and New Year's Eve. An admission fee is charged.

LA CROSSE

The city of La Crosse is a geologic oddity, escaping the crush of the glaciers that flattened most of Wisconsin several aeons ago. Since the pancaking effect of all that 1-mile-high ice missed the La Crosse vicinity, cliffs, gullies, ridges, and valleys abound. The 600-foot-high Grandad Bluff overlooks the city, affording a peek at three states: Minnesota, Iowa, and Wisconsin. Contributing to the beauty of the area, three major rivers converge on La Crosse: the La Crosse, the Black, and the Mississippi.

Native Americans appreciated the watery connection, as did early white explorers. In 1680 a canoeload of Frenchmen led by Friar Louis Hennepin marked out the location of what would eventually become the city of La Crosse. Permanent Anglo settlement started in 1841 when Nathan Myrick built the first cabin there. The site is now in the city's Pettibone Park. The town received its name from the Indian game of lacrosse, in which long racquets resembling a cross were used to batter a ball back and forth across a playing field.

Over the years the riverfront was developed, and La Crosse became a major port and entryway into the frontier. It grew strong with the lumber industry, river commerce, and brewery. In fact, the world's largest six-pack stands outside the **G. Heileman Brewing Company** at 1111 South Third Street. The bright-white holding tanks are emblazoned with the company's Old Style logo. For information on tours call (608) 782–2337. Parents can sip a brew in the hospitality room, while kids can enjoy a soft drink. The brewery's free tours are offered hourly 8:00 A.M. to 4:00 P.M.

Mondays through Saturdays from May through September. They are also available at 10:00 A.M. and 2:00 and 3:00 P.M. Mondays through Saturdays from October through April.

So what's to do here?

Plenty. Witness this partial lineup of family-oriented events: **Mardi Gras** in February, the **Coon Creek Canoe Race** at the end of April, the **Reggae Sunsplash** in mid-May, **June Dairy Days** and the **Seafood Fest** (in conjunction with the **American Bass Classic**) in June, **Riverfest** in July, the **La Crosse Interstate Fair** in mid-July, **Art Fair on the Green** at the end of August, the **Great River Festival of Traditional Jazz** on an early August weekend, the **Festival of Lanterns** (when lighted lanterns are floated down the Mississippi in the name of peace) in August, **Thunderfest** (five nights of fireworks at the **International Fireworks Festival**) in August, **Great River Traditional Music and Crafts Festival** at the end of August and beginning of September, the **Holiday Folk Fair** in November, and a vast menu of other activities. Better check with the La Crosse Convention and Visitors Bureau, Box 1895, Riverside Park, La Crosse 54602 (800–658–9424).

Tell the kids to keep a watch out for the giant carved eagle that stands in **Riverside Park,** site of many of the festivals and events sponsored by the city. Carved by local artist Elmer Peterson, the bald eagle, with its outstretched wings, is atop a 35-foot-high pillar. It is a tribute to Old Abe, a mascot of the state's famous Iron Brigade, which fought in the Civil War. In fact, often spotted from the vantage point of Riverside Park, are real bald eagles, drifting on the wind high above the Mississippi River.

For viewing other animals **Myrick Park Zoo** (608–789–7190) specializes in North American species rather than the exotic. Kids, however, love the antics of the spider monkeys on Monkey Island, a constant reminder of a kindergarten class at full steam. The zoo is tucked into the heart of a city park on the south side of the city, on La Crosse Street opposite the University of Wisconsin–La Crosse campus. In 1994 the park installed an extensive playground adjacent to the zoo with slides, rope swings, and jungle gym. Sometimes it is hard to tell who is having more fun: the kids or the monkeys.

The zoo is open 9:00 A.M. to 3:00 P.M. daily during the winter and

8:00 A.M. to dusk from April through late autumn. There are no lights in the park, so the place closes when the evening's bats and bugs begin flitting overhead. Holiday hours vary depending on staffing availability. There is no admission fee.

Take the time to stop at the **La Crosse Clock Company,** 125 South Second Street (608–782–8200), with its more than 1,000 timepieces. Cuckoo, alarm, grandfather, wall, and mantel clocks all tick-tock their merry way in the shop across from the Radisson Hotel and the Civic Center in downtown La Crosse. This is just the place to stock up for everybody in the family who is late with homework, runs overtime in the bathroom, or habitually misses the school bus because "the alarm didn't work." The store is open year-round 10:00 A.M. to 6:00 P.M. Mondays through Fridays and 10:00 A.M. to 5:00 P.M. Saturdays.

With all these new timepieces in the trunk, there's no excuse to miss the departure of the *Island Girl* dinner cruise at 7:30 P.M. nightly from the dock adjacent to American Marine and the Holiday Inn (on Highways 14/61). The company offers five different cruises daily from the end of April through October. At prices beginning at $9.95, the expeditions range from regular sightseeing excursions to romantic moonlight voyages. Since the company builds boats, passengers get to experience a new vessel at the start of every season. Call (608) 784–0556 for reservations. Or take a cruise sometime between May and late October on the *La Crosse Queen* (608–784–8523). The paddle-wheeler has a variety of sight-seeing expeditions and dinner cruises up and down the Mississippi. Prices for adults on the sightseeing cruise are $7.95, and $26 for a Saturday dinner cruise. Prices vary according to age and cruise. The boat dock is at Riverside Park, on the west end of State Street in downtown La Crosse.

Outdoor recreation opportunities are plentiful in the La Crosse area, using the city as a jumping-off point for biking, hiking, skiing, canoeing, and other fun. The Black and La Crosse rivers are popular with paddlers, who have also discovered Coon Creek and the Mississippi River and its backwaters. The last might be difficult for beginning canoeists, especially for kids, because of the current and underwater obstructions. So start on the rivers and graduate to the more difficult waterways as the family members gain experience. There are dozens of rental and sales outlets throughout

The stern-wheeler La Crosse Queen *offers 1 ½-hour sight-seeing cruises, Captain's Brunch cruises, and a Four Hour Cruise featuring a swing bridge, a lock, and a wildlife refuge.*
(Courtesy La Crosse Queen Cruises)

the region, supplying everything from anchors to bug spray to life preservers.

The La Crosse area is a cycler's image of dying and going to heaven. The major state bike trails meander through the region, combining urban and rural experience geared to the interests of all ages. **The Great River Trail** begins in Onalaska near La Crosse's far north side and rolls about 22 miles along the Mississippi River. The **La Crosse River Bicycle Trail** is a 21½-mile expedition paralleling the La Crosse River. The route cuts along farm pastures, streams, and maple groves. This trail connects with the **Elroy–Sparta Trail** and the **Great River State Trail.** There is plenty of camping along the routes, most of which are on hard-surface crushed rock along old railroad beds.

Approximately 100 miles of snowmobile trails crisscross La Crosse County, eventually hooking up with another 650 miles in the surrounding region. Seven local snowmobile clubs ensure that the trails are groomed to what seem to be interstate highway specifications. To receive maps, call the La Crosse Convention and Visitors Bureau at the number above.

For cross-country skiing **Bluebird Springs Recreation Area,** N2833 Smith Valley Road (608–781–2267), has 25 miles of groomed trails open during daylight hours. **Goose Island Park** (608–785–9770) near downtown also has excellent groomed paths. The **Hixon Forest Nature Center,** 2702 Quarry Road (608–784–0303), presents about 5 miles of trail through heavy woods and along high ridges. The **La Crosse County Forest Preserve,** just before the town of Burr Oak (608–788–0044), and **Mount La Crosse** (608–788–0044 in Wisconsin; 800–426–3665 outside Wisconsin), 6 miles south of downtown La Crosse, also have cross-country opportunities. The latter also has downhill skiing, with instructions and rentals.

As evidenced by all this activity, La Crosse in winter certainly isn't just a sit-inside place. Bundle up the tykes and take them on a sleigh ride at the **Sunset Riding Stables,** Route 2, W4803 Meyer Road (608–788–6629). During the snow season rides for two to eighty persons can be reserved each evening of the week. So bring all the cousins, grandparents, great-uncles, and Aunt Matilda for some extended-family frosty fun. Longjohns and heavy mittens are necessary. To keep their patrons from turning into snowfolks, a warming house is open en route to take off some of the chill. Bonfires for late-night fun are also possible. During other times of the year, the fee for riding is $9.00 an hour.

MILTON

Blackhawk Family Campground, off Rock County Y in Milton, has 295 sites with water and electricity and 110 tent campsites that can be rented by the day or the season. Swimming, fishing, canoe and boat rentals, hiking and biking trails, and shuffleboard, volleyball, and horseshoes are among the activities on the grounds. Dad and Mom will be glad for inside showers and toilets and an adult lounge. The kids can then play in the game room, where movies are also shown. Call (608) 868–2586.

MINERAL POINT

One of several cities in southwestern Wisconsin that owes its birth to the mining industry, Mineral Point is the third oldest community in the state. Founded by Cornish miners in 1827, it is now home to **Pendarvis**

(608–987–2122). The complex of historical buildings is operated by the State Historical Society of Wisconsin. It is open 9:00 A.M. to 5:00 P.M. daily from early May through early October. There is an admission fee, but children under five years of age are free. Senior citizens (sixty-five and over) receive a twenty percent discount. The last tour begins one hour before closing.

The name "Pendarvis" came from an estate in Cornwall near where many of the original settlers emigrated from. Called Cousin Jacks and Cousin Jennies, they brought valuable hard-rock skills with them as the tin mines in Cornwall petered out. They were also expert stonemasons and built homes like they had back in Cornwall, many of which were constructed in a valley near the mouth of the mines. This cluster of houses now forms the bulk of the Pendarvis complex. After 1847, however, lead prices and mining declined. Subsequently, Mineral Point lost much of its population as the settlers turned to farming. Others headed west to join the great gold rush. Within several generations most of the buildings had deteriorated, but in 1935 Robert Neal and Edgar Hellum purchased one old cottage and restored it. Over the following years they secured more properties and gradually expanded the restorations. The state historical society took over the site in 1971.

Here's a tip for parents tired of yelling for kids at suppertime. Do what the folks here used to do more than one hundred years ago. Along Shake Rag Under the Hill Street, the miners' wives used to flap a dishtowel or apron out an upper window or doorway so their husbands could see that the meal was ready. The fellows would come running to catch a bit of Cornish pasty, a traditional meat pie, before returning to work.

The community has become a center for the crafts industry, with numerous potters, weavers, and other artisans happy to show how they work. Among them are Jean Bohlin, a self-taught needlepointer; Solveig Nielsen, whose contemporary wool rugs and wall hangings touch on her Danish heritage; Kathleen Nutter, who specializes in handwoven chenille scarves; porcelain artists Diana and Tom Johnston; and photographer Mary North Allen. Several special events throughout the year should be fun for the family—ranging from **Pendarvis Founders' Day** at the end of May to the **Flavours of Old Cornwall,** a food fest in June that features traditional favorites such as saffron cake and clotted cream. On several weekends in August and September, youngsters can enjoy the **Drolls of Old Cornwall,** when storytellers relate drolls, or Cornish folk tales. The sessions, held in the Kiddleywink Pub, are free. Have the kids ask if there are still any tommyknockers down in the mines. These were Cornish fairies who supposedly could cause all sorts of trouble under the ground if an occasional offering of a portion of a miner's lunch wasn't made to them.

MONROE

Wilkommen to **Cheese Days** in downtown Monroe, held the third weekend in September in even-numbered years. The festival has been a tradition here since 1914, although the cheese industry got its kick-start in 1868. The limestone underlying the soil was perfect for pastures and provided the right grasses for happy Holsteins and Brown Swiss cows. Paying tribute to the major industry in Green County, the Cheese Days activities bring together farmers, dairy workers, big city folk, college students, and everyone in between. It is a big family reunion, and there's nothing cheesy about this party, with its Cheesemaker's Ball, children's parade, street dancing, concessions, carnival, arts and crafts show, cheesemaking demonstrations, and, of course, tons of cheese sandwiches. A cheese sale tent offers up a range of dairy goodies, from Swiss to Muenster. Cheese factory and farm tours aboard buses depart every hour from the northeast corner of the town square (kids eight and under are free).

Hearkening back to chese country's Swiss heritage, there is plenty of yodeling and alpine music. The **Cheese Days Chase** consists of 20,000-, 10,000-, and 5,000-meter runs for different age categories. For information about Cheese Days, write to the festival offices, Box 606, Monroe 53566.

Take the kids on a cheese hunt around the Monroe area, if all that partying isn't enough. Here are a few of the licensed cheese factories that are open for touring: **Gold Brick Cheese Co.** (608–922–6252), Gratiot; **Zimmerman Cheese Co.** (608–968–3414), Wiota; **Valley View Cheese Co-op** (608–439–5569), South Wayne; **Wood–Andrews Cheese Co-op** (608–439–5524), South Wayne; **Chula Vista Cheese Co.** (608–439–5211), Browntown; **Davis Cheese** (608–966–3361), Browntown; **Curran Cheese, Inc.** (608–966–3452), Browntown; **Whitehead**

Cheese Co-op (608–325–3522), Monroe; **Deppeler Cheese Factory** (608–325–6311), Monroe; **Franklin Cheese Co-op** (608–325–3725), Monroe; and **Green County Cheese Co-op** (608–325–4346), Monroe. For a more complete listing, contact the Cheese Days folks at the address above.

NEILLSVILLE

Three miles west of Neillsville on State Highway 10 is a picturesque ridge overlooking three counties of south/southwestern Wisconsin. It is quiet here, with only the breeze making any noise as it tinkles the dog tags on a memorial dedicated to the Wisconsin dead of Vietnam. This is the **Highground,** the Vietnam Veterans' Memorial Park, visited by thousands of vets each year to heal themselves. It is a hushed place, where even the most bubbly youngsters will feel the presence of something larger than themselves. The focal point of the memorial is a life-size bronze sculpture showing three soldiers and a sheltering nurse; it was made by Wisconsin artist Robert A. Kanyusik. A wind chime is comprised of 1,215 tags, marking each of the state's dead and the thirty-seven still missing in action. An earthen mound in the shape of a peace dove is at the base of the bluff, in memory of all prisoners of war and MIAs. In the center of the dove is soil from all seventy-two counties in Wisconsin. The memorial is accessible all the time year-round. For more information call (715) 743–4224.

In Neillsville the kids will also be sobered to see the **1897 Clark County Jail Museum** (715–743–3655). The fortresslike building at 215 East Fifth Street is listed on the National Register of Historic Places. Thick walls, turrets, and guard stations demonstrate that this was certainly not a country club. Tours include a peek into the sheriff's office and cell blocks. The last live-in sheriff and his family departed the premises in 1974, but the cells continued to be used until 1978, when a more modern structure was built. Entering the building is a surprise because tours start in the sheriff's old residence, containing a parlor, a sitting room, and other homey accommodations. An open stairway leads upstairs, where the children of the family stayed and played. But the jail portion of the structure is totally different. The massive cell doors, the peekholes for viewing prisoners, the exercise area, and the commodes in the corner of each tiny cell testify to the security-conscious nature of the place. The sections that held women and juveniles now hold a bright display of flags, a sewing room, an antique telephone office, and an old-time barber shop—all of which softens the edges. The jail is open from the third Sunday in May and closes on Labor Day weekend. Hours are 1:00 to 4:00 P.M. Saturdays and Sundays. Admission is $1.50 for adults and $1.00 for students.

NEW GLARUS

Another of the Swiss-founded communities in southern Wisconsin, New Glarus looks as if it was cut from a picture postcard of the home country. In a way it was, because the settlers found the wonderful rolling green hills reminiscent of their original cantons. Subsequently, their outbuildings, farms, and residences had all the look of the alpine world from which they came in 1845. This heritage is preserved in the **Swiss Historical Village Museum** at 612 Seventh Avenue (608–527–2317), where twelve pioneer buildings have been refurbished and are now open for touring. Youngsters can touch the early farming implements, learn how cheese was made, and talk with guides about Wisconsin pioneer life. The museum is open 9:00 A.M. to 5:00 P.M. daily May through October. Admission is charged.

A stop at the **Chalet of the Golden Fleece Museum,** 618 Second Street (608–527–2614), will put more of that history into perspective for kids who need additional research on the ethnic history of the community. Carved wooden craft items, early table settings, and similar homey artifacts are preserved there in a building constructed in typical Bernese style, with wooden shutters and fountains of red and white carnations overflowing from window boxes. The chalet is open 9:00 A.M. to 4:30 P.M. daily between early May and the end of October. Admission is charged.

Everywhere in town the Swiss flag proudly flies next to the U.S. flag. Be sure the kids know that the design of the Red Cross flag was adapted from that of the traditionally neutral Swiss, with their red banner and its white cross leading to the social service organization's white banner and crimson cross.

Lace making was a traditional craft carried from Switzerland by many of the pioneer women, who excelled at its intricacies. The **Swiss Miss Lace Factory,** 1100 Second Street (608–527–2515), has extensive displays of old patterns. Today's youngsters can watch how modern lace is made, however, when the looms imported from Switzerland are in full operation. The factory is open at no charge from 8:00 A.M. to 4:00 P.M. daily. For special sales and bargains, the firm's outlet store is only a short stroll—2 blocks east of the factory.

When the kids get antsy waiting for Mom to finish looking over the lace selections, it's time to take them out to the **Sugar River State Trail** (608–527–2334). The trail is a 23-mile biking/hiking pathway guaranteed to build up calves and get the youngsters busy pumping pedals. The trail is built on an abandoned railroad bed and even goes through a covered bridge. There are easy grades and long, flat distances, so little kids can do well if nobody rushes. If a family hasn't brought bikes along on vacation, cycles can be rented at the trailhead offices at 418 Railroad Street.

The community is proud of its Swiss heritage and sponsors numerous festivals and ethnic events. Announcing the start of many of the programs is a local musician blowing into his sonorous alpine horn, formerly used in the mountains to call the cowherds. The horn is so long that its mouth rests on the ground. The sound is as meaningful to the Swiss as the skirl of bagpipes is to the Scots and just as distinctive. Among events that entire families will find enjoyable are the **New Glarus Swiss Polkafest** in late May, the **New Glarus Community Festival** also in May, the **Little Switzerland Festival** in June, and the **Heidi Craft and Art Fair** in late June. In early August New Glarus celebrates **Volkfest,** the Swiss Independence Day. The New Glarus **Octoberfest** in early October and the annual **Chamber Antique Show & Sale** in late October also attract visitors from around Wisconsin and northern Illinois.

Volunteer, amateur actors and actresses star in the *Heidi* drama each June, bringing to life the popular children's story about the little girl of the mountains. These productions are especially geared to eager, attentive youngsters in the audience. Then early in September the city stages its *Wilhelm Tell* drama. The play touches on the well-known story about the patriot forced to shoot an apple from his son's head by means of a bow and arrow. Naturally, Tell does well, the uninjured young son is freed, and the nasty, despotic sheriff is eventually deposed. The Friday and Sunday productions are performed in English, while the Saturday show is staged in German.

To confirm dates for any of these festivals and performances, call the New Glarus Visitor and Convention Bureau (608–527–2095). What's best, dad or mom don't need to yodel to get reservations. Just ask for details.

PEPIN

This lake community is the birthplace of Laura Ingalls Wilder, author of the popular "Little House" series of children's books. Pepin has named its city park in her honor, and a memorial has been erected there as well. The **Pepin Historical Museum,** 3076 Third Street (715–442–3161), emphasizes Wilder's prodigious literary legacy. The free museum is open 10:00 A.M. to 5:00 P.M. daily from May 15 to October 15. Seven miles northwest of town, on County CC, the Little House Wayside sits on a three-acre site that includes a reproduction of the cabin she wrote about in *Little House in the Big Woods.* Suggest to the gang that they turn their minds inward and imagine Pa and Ma coming out of the tiny house, along with all the other characters made famous in Wilder's delightful stories. The wayside is open year-round. There is no charge.

POTOSI

The city of Potosi is the Catfish Capital of Wisconsin, with a **Catfish Festival** held each July, celebrating the wonderful, nutritious—but ugly as day-old sin—fish that plops around in the nearby Mississippi River. Potosi was once larger than Chicago and Milwaukee—in the late 1820s, when lead was discovered in the bluffs overlooking the rolling river. Thousands of miners flocked to the hills, setting up camps all along a deep valley that cuts into the heart of lead country. The **St. John Lead Mine** (608–763–2121) on Highway 133 was one of the deepest and most profitable mines. Park near the A-frame, where owners Mr. and Mrs. Harry Henderson live; climb up the steep stairs; and enter the dim, cool interior. Lights along the way show the pick and chisel marks made by men working for hours on their backs or on hands and knees to recover the precious lead. When the miners first arrived, they burrowed into the hills to seek shelter from the rain and cold. Their refuges reminded one visitor of badger holes, and hence the nickname of Wisconsin was born: the Badger State. The mine is open May through mid-October from 9:00 A.M. to 5:00 P.M. daily. There is an admission fee.

Only the village of Potosi remains of what were once several communities stretching along the valley floor, each named for its respective ethnic group, such as British Hollow. The town was originally called Snake Hollow, and *Ripley's Believe It or Not* claimed that in its heyday the 5-mile-long main road was the longest street in the United States without an intersection. A few ruined building foundations, shadows of the past, can still be seen, but that is all.

PRAIRIE DU CHIEN

Anyone who guesses the meaning of the town's name wins an ice-cream cone at the **St. Feriole Island Railroad,** an assortment of shops in a string of old railroad cars parked along the Mississippi River, just to the south of the Villa Louis mansion on the river frontage road. Just look for the line of railcars perched on the riverbank. Some historians say the city was named after a local Indian leader during frontier days. Others indicate it simply meant "field of dogs," referring to the hundreds of prairie dogs that were seen by the first French visitors in the 1600s. Since the meaning is really unclear, everyone should probably slurp a cone. Stand on the veranda behind the train cars and watch the river roll by while lapping up the vanilla or chocolate. The shops are open through the summer.

With its history Prairie du Chien is a must-stop on the exploration list. The **Fort Crawford Military Hospital,** 717 Beaumont Street (608–326–6960), was a major health-care center in the rugged days before the Civil War. The fort itself was built in 1816 and was the center of frontier military activity during the Black Hawk War. Dr. William Beaumont, a medical pioneer and surgeon, performed a famous experiment on a trapper who was injured in the stomach. The doctor covered the wound with a flap of skin so he was still able to watch the digestive process. Now a museum of medical history, the facility will amaze kids with all its rudimentary tools and drugs used by frontier doctors. It makes one appreciate the quick med stops, emergency clinics, and CAT-scans available everywhere in contemporary life.

Take the kids into the fort's **Stovall Hall of Health** to learn about their bodies from the Transparent Twins, life-size plastic female models. One shows the twenty-five organs of the body, and the other highlights the 200 bones in the skeletal system. Tape-recorded messages describe the function of each organ.

The **Villa Louis** mansion, 521 Villa Louis Road (608–326–2721), is on the banks of the Mississippi River. A state historical site, it is open 9:00 A.M. to 5:00 P.M. daily May through October. It shows how a wealthy frontier family used to live. Admission is charged. Steve says he's always been proud to visit Villa Louis because his great-great-grandmother, Bridget O'Malley, was a linen maid there in the mid-1800s when she emigrated from Ireland.

Prairie du Chien annually hosts a **Fur Traders Rendezvous** on St. Feriole Island near Villa Louis on the third weekend in June. Grizzled mountain men, Native American trappers, and appropriately garbed military men from the era fill the grounds with their tents and tepees. They lay out trade goods, talk shop, cook over open fires, scratch, and look at guests from the twentieth century with amusement. Of course, when the weekend is over, they all go back to being bank presidents, mechanics, nurses, shop owners, and lawyers. The kids can barter for knicknacks and come away with pelts, muskets, tomahawks, and flint—if it will all fit in the car. Call the Prairie du Chien Chamber of Commerce (608–326–8555) for details of the free event, or drop in at their offices at 211 South Main Street. They are open during usual weekday business hours.

There are several commercial fishermen in town who offer freshly caught snapping turtle, catfish, and carp for hungry visitors. Hunks of smoked catfish, along with crackers, are especially great for munching while trekking overland. And be sure to pick up some squeaky cheese curds, Wisconsin's favorite snack, to go along with the catfish for a true gourmet picnic. Load up on napkins before heading out of town because sticky fingers are generally the result. For details on such outlets, contact the Prairie du Chien Chamber of Commerce.

TREMPEALEAU

Two miles west of Trempealeau on Park Road, off Wisconsin Highway 35, is **Perrot State Park** (608–534–6409), named after a French explorer who wandered through the neighborhood in 1665. The park is atop 500-foot-high bluffs overlooking the juncture of the Mississippi and the Trempealeau rivers. The peaks were considered a sacred area by the Native Americans. Early explorers used the landmarks as they journeyed westward. Several burial and ceremonial mounds built by prehistoric Indians can be found in the park. Get the kids to look over the mounds and discuss what type of people must have made them and why. The park is open 8:00 A.M. to 11:00 P.M. Park stickers are required.

Four miles north of the park is the **Trempealeau National Wildlife Refuge** (608–539–2311), managed by the U.S. Fish and Wildlife Service. The refuge is at the junction of West Prairie and Refuge roads, just off Wisconsin Highway 35. Look for directional signs at all the intersections. There is no way that anyone could see the entire 6,000 acres of the refuge in a weekend or even a week, but take the kids on the 5-mile self-guided auto tour around the park. There are also a well-marked, ½-mile nature trail and a marsh to explore. Whitetail deer, bald eagles, ducks, geese, and other creatures can readily be seen. The refuge is open to public during daylight hours, with the office open 7:30 A.M. to 4:00 P.M. Mondays through Fridays year-round.

VIROQUA

Viroqua's Double Daze Twin Contest during its **Heritage Fest** (608–637–8727) each June brings twins from around the Midwest to participate in the fun, which includes a parade, a classic car show, and a gem show. Entrants are judged in different age divisions, from toddler to old-timers. Rules are simple: Whoever looks most alike or most unalike wins. Small plaques are handed out to the victors. The contest participants also get a free breakfast and a ride in the parade.

Held in Viroqua during September is the **Vernon County Fair** (608–637–3165), the final county fair of the season in Wisconsin. Harness racing is the big event, with top horses from around the Midwest thundering around the turns. Take the kids back by the stables to watch the grooming and other preparations for the events. Sometimes a driver will let a youngster sit atop a sulky to get a feel for the cart's size and light weight. Then stroll through the exhibit buildings to watch the slicer-dicer-chopper salesmen, talk with implement dealers, stare at the county's largest pigs, and admire the 4-H birdhouses and aprons. And eat . . . and eat . . . and eat. Corn on the cob, hamburgers, chili dogs, cotton candy, homemade pie, roast beef dinners. Ah, that's the country fair. There is a small admission fee.

WESTBY

On the weekend closest to May 17, downtown Westby holds a three-day celebration of Norway's Constitution Day. Called **Syttende Mai,** the activities include a troll hunt for kids, a huge quilt auction, arts and crafts exhibits, music, and dancing. A Sunday afternoon parade showcases the Scandinavian heritage of the community. For details call (608) 634–4193.

Westby is also an outdoors town, with the **Snowflake Annual Ski Jumping Tournament** (608–634–2002) in February, held at the Westby Ski Club's Nordic Center (north of town off State Highway 27 on Vernon County P). The 65-meter run's landing zone converts to a nine-hole, par-three golf course in the summer. This is not something for the little kids to try off the roof of the house into a snowbank, but they'll get a thrill out of watching the international pros sailing through the air. Tickets are $8.00 in advance and $10.00 at the gate.

WOODFORD

Although kids can have a wonderful time visiting **Black Hawk Memorial Park** (608–465–3390) along Sand Road and Lafayette County Highway Y near Woodford, they should know the history of the park to appreciate a little bit more of Wisconsin's history. The park, with its hook-shaped Bloody Lake, was the site of a battle in 1832 in which outnumbered Sac and Fox Indians under Chief Black Hawk fought frontier militia and regular army troops. Later that year, the Sac were slaughtered while trying to surrender to the U.S. Cavalry at Bad Axe in Vernon County, along the Mississippi River. In 1990 Governor Tommy Thompson formally apologized to the descendants of the Sac Nation for what had happened in that long-ago time. The governor's statements marked the first time that any governmental representative apologized to Native Americans for war crimes committed against their ancestors.

Tree-shaded Black Hawk Memorial Park is quiet now, although a rendezvous with trapper and trader reenactors is held annually the first weekend of May, complete with black-powder musket shoots and tomahawk throwing. There is a boat landing leading into the slow-moving east branch of the Pecatonica River, where bass, catfish, and trout lurk. Primitive camping is allowed at $5.00, but there are no sewer, water, or electric hookups available. Kids love it. The park is open daily 6:00 A.M. to midnight year-round. From April through October, there is an admission of $1.00.

GREATER MILWAUKEE– SOUTHEAST

lease, don't constantly bring up the brewery scene to Milwaukeeans. Even in the heyday of the hops, beer making was way down the scale on the city's economic base. But OK, nobody will reeeeeaaaally mind if a guest calls this city Beertown. After all, an image is an image.

So over a draft think also of pro hockey and soccer, poetry slams, ballet, alternative theater, Gallery Nights, enough museums to fill a shelf of guidebooks, magnificent eateries, race cars, dog tracks, ethnic festivals, and charter fishing for lunker German brown trout. Now that is a vacation menu.

So there are brewery tours. Go on 'em and enjoy yourselves (soda for the kids, mind you), but then head for a fantastic Sicilian restaurant, the Florentine Opera, or a hands-on kids' Discovery World adventure museum. This is the doing place of the state, where urbanity can be realized without being overwhelming.

Lakes, parks, and green space make southeastern Wisconsin a delightfully special place where no one hungers for scenic vistas. Nor will stomachs rumble for long: Grits and corned beef, Polish sausage and boiled codfish, apple pie, and frozen custard—you can feed the most demanding family, even one with widely different culinary demands.

You gotta be here to believe it all.

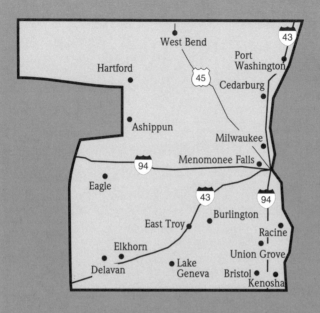

West Bend

Hartford

Port
Washington

Cedarburg

Ashippun

Milwaukee

Menomonee Falls

Eagle

East Troy

Burlington

Racine

Elkhorn

Lake
Geneva

Union Grove

Delavan

Bristol

Kenosha

Greater Milwaukee–Southeast

ASHIPPUN

For a honey of a museum, sample a variety of the bee's sweet stuff at **Honey Acres,** located on Highway 67 in Ashippun (414–474–4411). The museum is free. It is open 9:00 A.M. to 3:30 P.M. weekdays year-round. From May 15 to October 31, Honey Acres is also open from noon to 4:00 P.M. on weekdays. The facility is closed on holidays. The youngsters will learn everything they ever needed to know about the buzzers and bee-keeping. Exhibits in the museum include a series of spigots that drip clover and other types of honey for a tempting tastebud treat.

BRISTOL

Thundering hooves, the clash of steel upon steel, and merry minstrel tunes make for all the stuff of fantasy, fable, and kids' dreams. That's the Bristol **Renaissance Faire** (414–396–4320), where those dreams do come alive from the end of June through August. The actors and actresses who play the roles of knight, princess, beggar, or king certainly get into the swing of things, thus making the scenes very realistic. From jousting to juggling, from banquet table to royal court, the fair sweeps up its guests and plunks them down in another era. The grounds, with all their flag-snapping pageantry, are located at 12420 128th Street, about a half-hour's drive from downtown Kenosha. As they say at the fair, "Eat, drynke, and be merrie." It's enough to make a kid want to scurry to the library for an added dose of Arthur and the Round Table. Hours are 10:00 A.M. to 7:00 P.M. June 24 to August 20. Admission is $14.00 for adults and $6.50 for youngsters five to twelve years of age. Kids under age five are free.

BURLINGTON

For a kicked-back, relaxing ride in old-time style, gallop up to **Kane's Circle K Coach & Carriage,** 27535 Ketterhagen Drive in Burlington (414–534–2771). Draft horses the size of, well, Belgians and Percherons, if not elephants, pull haywagons, sleighs, stagecoaches, and covered wagons around the farm's meandering trails. The ranch also offers elegant carriage rides in downtown Lake Geneva during the summer when the weather permits. No need to fear the winter winds when Mr. Frosty sweeps down out of the North. Monster lap robes are provided for sleigh rides, perfect for wintry snuggling. Families just need to provide their own longjohns or red woolies.

Designated Chocolate City USA by the Wisconsin state legislature—a sweet kudo indeed—Burlington is home of a Nestlé Company chocolate factory. This is reason enough for the city to host a giant **Chocolate Festival** each year on grounds 1 block east of State Highway 36, with parking on Maryland Avenue. Held annually the third weekend in May, the free event consists of a parade, musical entertainment (past performers have included Blood, Sweat, and Tears and similar major names) and kids' entertainment featuring magicians and a petting zoo. On display is the world's largest milk chocolate sculpture, which usually tops out at more than 2,000 pounds. Dinosaurs, castles, and giant crunch bars have been subjects of chocolate artists in the past. No nibbling is allowed on the statues, but there is always plenty of chocolate that can be eaten because candy bars are freely passed out. Service clubs, nonprofit organizations, and restaurants always sell calorie-sinful chocolate desserts to go along with the other fare at their booths. For details contact the Burlington Area Chamber of Commerce, 112 East Chestnut Street (414–763–6044).

The **Kiwanis Pancake Breakfast and Family Fair,** held in late February each year at Cooper School, 249 Conkey Street, can help tummies prepare for the summer chocolate extravaganza. Might as well start training early with syrup and butter. For adults, the breakfast is $3.75 at the door, with children under age twelve at $2.50. Call (414) 763–2555 for details on the kids' activities, which are the nucleus of the event.

If that isn't enough to get the kids twirling, take them over to the **Spinning Top Exploratory Museum,** which exhibits more than 1,000 antique and modern tops. Add gyroscopes and tons of yo-yos and there's enough here to keep a tyke interested for several hours. Free demonstrations by champ yo-yo-ists show what can be done without knocking oneself on the head. Everyone is encouraged to try his or her own hands-on experiment. Of course, there is a museum gift shop, with all shapes, sizes, colors, and styles of tops. The museum is located at 533 Milwaukee Avenue (414–763–3946 or 728–5623). Hours are by primarily by appointment only because tours take 90 minutes and the staff enjoys working one-on-one with the visitors. Every three months, new hours are listed for drop-by traffic. The facility was extensively remodeled in early 1995.

Only 8 miles east of Burlington near Kansasville is the **Bong State Recreation Area,** (414–878–5600) on State Highway 142, which offers camping, hiking, and plenty of fishing for walleye, perch, bass, and northern pike. A swimming beach there is great for little ones wishing to splash around the shallows and pretend that toes are nibbled by underwater creatures. Cross-country skiing, horseback riding, snowmobiling, hunting, and even a sled-dog training area round out the recreational opportunities at Bong. During the summer rangers conduct interpretive programs, describing the local flora and fauna. Numerous hot-air balloonists also find the Bong area perfect for liftoff points, with southeastern Wisconsin's flat land easy for the chase cars. The sprawling recreation site, which is open year-round, was named for Richard Bong, an air ace who died during World War II.

CEDARBURG

The annual **Strawberry Festival** held at the end of June in Cedarburg is always a berry fun time for families. Sample luscious strawberry desserts, take part in the strawberry-pie-eating contests, and try the berry-bob competition. There is also plenty of music and stage entertainment. Visitors are encouraged to attend the free festival and purchase all the strawberry delights they wish from the vendors and shops. A folk art show, featuring more than fifty Midwest artists, is a popular draw during the festival weekend. For more information call (414) 377–8020 or (800) 827–8020.

The festival is centered on the **Cedar Creek Settlement** in the historic village, a jump back to the mid-1800s when the town was born. While in the neighborhood, visit the old **Cedarburg Woolen Mill** (414–377–0345), at the corner of Bridge Road and Washington Avenue, which now houses a warren of craft shops, art galleries, and similar trendy retail outlets. The original textile machinery, dating from the 1860s, is situated around the complex for a rustic look. It's a good idea to show the kids how cloth was made a century ago before turning them loose inside the building, with its numerous staircases and hide-and-seek hallways.

The **Cedar Creek Winery,** with a tasting room in the mill, is open year-round 10:00 A.M. to 5:00 P.M. Mondays through Saturdays and noon to 5:00 P.M. Sundays. There is no admission charge, so we've always saved our coins, scanned the racks looking for a good pinot noir or chenin blanc, and indulged in a vintage to take home for the wine rack. Call (414) 377–8020. The winery is one of America's most noted small regional wineries and provides a chance to learn how vintners create their fine wines just like back home in Europe. The shop hosts a **Winery Open House** on the third full weekend in March, with special tastings and lectures on wine production, as well as a grape-stomping contest for purple-footers. White socks for participants are not encouraged.

Regardless of the season—even in the frostiest weather—the mill and winery, as well as the rest of Cedarburg, always bustle. A **Winter Festival** is staged the first full weekend in February, with bed races on the millpond, along with snow- and ice-sculpting competitions and indoor dramatic and musical entertainment. A **Wine and Harvest Festival** is held on the third full weekend in September, with pumpkin carvers, hayrides, wine tasting, blacksmiths pounding on forges, and music. For more information call the winery at the number given above.

Just a short walk from the mill is Cedarburg's downtown **Cultural Center,** which features permanent and temporary exhibitions exploring the community's history, heritage, and contemporary culture. The center is free, open 10:00 A.M. to 5:00 P.M. Tuesdays through Saturdays and 1:00 to 5:00 P.M. Sundays. Call (414) 375–3767 for details on programs, shows, and exhibits. On Sunday afternoons in July, the center also sponsors an outdoor concert series on the lawn of City Hall, where visitors can sprawl on the grass and relax. Kids are welcome to turn somersaults, play tag, and, of course, listen to the music. On the stroll to the center, shoppers are lured by the antiques shops, boutiques, and galleries lining the main street. For more information on Cedarburg and its festivals, call (414) 375–3676.

A must-stop to satisfy any sweet tooth in the crew is **Beerntsen's Candies,** W61 N520 Washington Ave (414–377–9512), with its hand-dipped chocolates. The homemade hard candies, brittles, and fudge are worth walking across Wisconsin for, to say nothing of the caramel corn and roasted nuts. Located in an old stagecoach inn, Beerntsen's has been a Cedarburg tradition since 1932. The candy shop is open year-round on Mondays through Saturdays from 10:00 A.M. to 6:00 P.M. and Sundays from noon until 4:00 P.M.

Stock up on goodies for a walk in **Covered Bridge Park,** where the kids can run though the last remaining original covered bridge in Wisconsin. There is a comfortable picnic area alongside the bridge, which spans Cedar Creek. Take Washington Avenue north to Five Corners, then continue to the park via Covered Bridge Road. It's about a half-hour's leisurely drive from downtown Cedarburg.

DELAVAN

Between 1847 and 1894 Delavan, the Sawdust City, was home to some twenty-six circuses, which had winter quarters here. The Spring Grove and St. Andrew's cemeteries in town have dozens of gravesites marking the final resting place of roustabouts, clowns, lion tamers, front-office workers, acrobats, and showgirls. A rearing elephant statue in the downtown square is a reminder of that center ring heritage and a perfect backdrop for family portraits. So don't forget the tripod and camera. Keeping all that fabulous, spangly Big Top tradition alive is the **Clown Hall of Fame and Research Center,** 114 North Third Street (414–728–9075). Regularly scheduled clown shows, workshops, and seminars show youngsters and oldsters what goes on behind the greasepaint, big rubber noses, and oversize shoes. A theater and exhibition hall, along with an auditorium, make up the complex. The museum honors outstanding clown performers and maintains a national archive of clown memorabilia and research material that is open to the public, whether they're kids doing term papers or more advanced scholars.

The facility is open 10:00 A.M. to 5:00 P.M. Mondays through Fridays and 10:00 A.M. to 4:00 P.M. Saturdays and Sundays in the summer. In the winter it is open 10:00 A.M. to 4:00 P.M. Mondays through Saturdays. Live clown shows are held at 11:00 A.M. on Saturdays throughout the year. Admission is $2.50 to view the museum on your own, with regulary scheduled guided tours at $7.00 for adults and $6.00 for seniors (sixty and over) and kids eighteen and under. Youngsters three and under free.

While in town, stop at **Earlene's Doll House,** 116 North Second Street (414–728–9500) to look over the collection of antique dolls and to check out the doll wigs, clothes, trunks, and patterns. If one of the youngsters has a broken doll, it can be repaired at Earlene's, which acts as an emergency clinic for tattered toys. The shop is open Tuesdays through Saturdays from 10:00 A.M. to 5:00 P.M. in the winter. From Memorial through Labor Day, it is also open on Sundays from noon to 5:00 P.M.

Kids will also engrossed by **Dam Road Bears** (414–728–9417), where they can watch toy bears being custom-made. Owner Gail Earle is a self-proclaimed "teddy artist," making more than 500 stuffed critters for sale every year. The shop, packed with fat little fuzzies, is located in an old barn, 1 mile north of Walworth Avenue on North Terrace Street near Lake Comus. "Bears" is open "by chance" or appointment. So call in advance.

EAGLE

In Eagle **Old World Wisconsin,** one of six living-history museums operated by the Wisconsin State Historical Society, consists of 576 acres of hills, forests, pastures, and cornfields in the southern unit of the Kettle Moraine State Forest. Buildings at Old World were collected from around the state and placed in their appropriate ethnic site, featuring German, Polish, Norwegian, and Danish farms, along with a crossroads Yankee village. Interpreters in period clothing perform the tasks done by rural residents in the nineteenth and early twentieth centuries. They care for the crops and rare breeds of animals in the same way as did the early Wisconsin farmers. It is not uncommon to see Cotswold sheep, Ossabaw hogs, Lineback cattle, and Morgan–Percheron horses.

Even the visitor center has historical significance, with the octagonal Clausing Barn (1897) now housing a cafeteria-style restaurant that offers simple fare at a decent price. A museum, restrooms, and a theater are in the adjacent Ramsey Barn, built in 1841 in Fort Atkinson. Horse-drawn wagons make regular loops around the grounds, picking up and dropping off families who can explore the farmsites, talk with the interpreters, and learn more about life on the frontier. Each cluster of buildings is authentic, right down to the original sauna on the Finnish farmsite. Kids enjoy poking around the Raspberry School, a one-room schoolhouse built in 1896 by three Scandinavian families in remote Bayfield County, near Lake Superior's Raspberry Bay.

The grounds often host special programs, ranging from traditional Fourth of July celebrations complete with political speeches to uplifting holiday caroling in tiny St. Peter's Church (1839), the first Catholic church built in Milwaukee. Cross-country skiing is allowed every Friday, Saturday, and Sunday from late December through the first weekend in March as conditions permit, with hot cider and cookies often served from kitchens at the various homesteads. The easy-to-difficult trails (they are marked as appropriate) loop and swish over the low hills, leading through the farmyards and even an open barn or two. Rentals of ski equipment are available in the Ramsey Barn, with lunches offered in the Clausing Barn. The last ski tickets of the day are sold at 3:30 P.M., so be sure to get on-site early enough to see as much as possible. It is an amazing sight to swoop down a maple-covered ridge with kids in tow and suddenly find the entire family in a different century. Something Twilight Zone–ish about it all, but you can't beat the educational, eye-opening fun.

Old World Wisconsin is located at S103 W37890 Highway 67 (414–594–2116). Eagle itself is only 35 miles from downtown Milwaukee, 55 miles from Madison, and 75 miles from Chicago, but stepping through the front gates is definitely moving into another life. Old World Wisconsin is open daily, generally from 10:00 A.M. to 4:00 P.M. Admission is $7.00 for adults and $6.30 for seniors sixty-five and older. Kids (ages five to twelve) are $3.00. Cross-country ski fees are $4.00 for adults and $2.00 for children on weekends only. Call for ski conditions.

The museum also hosts what it calls Homespun Journeys, packages that include tours and supper at Old World, an overnight stay at a local B&B and a visit to the East Troy Railroad Museum, just to the south.

EAST TROY

The **East Troy Electric Railroad Museum,** located at 200 Church Street in downtown East Troy brings back the fun of smooth, quiet travel on tracks that once linked small communities in southeastern Wisconsin with Milwaukee. Rides can be taken on vintage trolleys that scoot along over 10 miles of farmland. On Saturdays and Sundays from mid-September through the end of October, the trolley ride stops at the **Elegant Farmer market,** where passengers can stop off for a hayride, pick their own pumpkins and apples, or have the chance to make fresh caramel apples. Everyone can then pick up a later train for the return to East Troy. So if you happen to leave a kid behind while out looking for the Great Pumpkin, he or she will eventually show up.

The museum is staffed by volunteers who are always eager to explain the finer points of trolley travel. While a peek inside the repair barns might be oily and messy due to the work being done on the cars, it is a chance for kids to look at the inner workings of the machinery. Be sure they keep their hands to themselves, however, both for safety and cleanliness. Inside the old depot on Church Street can be found all sorts of memorabilia about the use of trolleys as commuter transportation.

Throughout the summer the trolley museum sponsors special programs, such as its annual **Trolley Festival** in May, **June Dairy Month** (with free ice cream with each paid fare), **Model Railroad Weekend** in July, **Dog Days of Summer** (with free hot dogs with each paid fare), and the **Fall Fun Days,** with their stop at the farmer's market. The number of the twenty-four-hour information line is (414) 548–ETER.

For winter fun in southeastern Wisconsin, the **Alpine Valley Resort,** on County Highway D off State Highway 20, offers twelve slopes serviced by eleven chairlifts and five rope tows. Saunas, pizza parlors, a cafeteria, lounges, and whirlpools make Alpine Valley the closest thing to Aspen in these Dairy State parts. KinderKids meet daily at 10:30 A.M. and 1:30 P.M. for lessons and bunny slope fun. ValleyKids is a six-week instructional program, starting in early January, for older youngsters wanting to perfect their skiing form. The resort also features an adult and youth race series, which also begins in January, along with NASTAR racing open to all ages on Saturdays and Sundays. Night skiing is available each evening until 11:00 P.M. Lift tickets for adults are $25 on the weekend and $20 on weekdays; kids' prices are several dollars less. Rentals of poles, boots, and skis are available beginning at $14 for kids on weekdays. Call the resort at (414) 642–7374.

ELKHORN

With plenty of bumps, whoops, and hollering, the **Wisconsin High School Rodeo,** held at the fairgrounds on the northeast side of Elkhorn, brings the Old West to southeastern Wisconsin at the end of May. Bareback bronco riding, girls' and boys' cutting, barrel racing, calf roping, breakaway roping, bull riding, team roping, saddle bronco riding, goat tying, steer wrestling, and pole bending are among the rootin'-tootin' events. Although there is an admission charge, kids under age five are admitted free. For details call (608) 794-2476. A country roundup dance at the Activity Center on the Walworth County Fairgrounds is held on the Saturday night of the rodeo. Of course, there are line dancing, plenty of polkas, and usually even a bit of vintage rock and roll.

Since kids are usually the apple of their grandparents' eye, have the kids host their grandads and grandmas at the annual **Grandparents Day** early in September at the Apple Barn (414–728–8810 or 728–3266) on Route 2 near Elkhorn. Take either County Trunk O or H north of the city to Sugar Creek Road. It's the kids' job to watch for the signs from then on

Would-be buckaroos test their mettle at the Wisconsin High School Rodeo. Events include barrel racing, steer wrestling, and bull riding. (Courtesy Mary Jo Schoonover)

along the highway. There is an apple pancake breakfast, along with pony rides, face painting, clowns, and a small animal display. There is no charge to visit the farm, and the breakfast is under $5.00. Later in the month is Happy Birthday, Johnny Day, in honor of Johnny Appleseed, followed in October by Apple Fest Weekend, Pumpkin Daze, and Sweetest Day. But whatever the celebration, there are always apples, apples, apples. The orchard has been in the same family since the 1840s and now grows almost twenty varieties of the juicy one-a-day-keeps-the-doc-away fruit, from Paulared to Northern Spy, along with pears and plums.

HARTFORD

The **Hartford Heritage Auto Museum,** 147 North Rural Street (414–673–7999), honors the memory of the old Kissel automobile, which was built in town between 1906 and 1931. Nash autos, also a Wisconsin-designed car, are displayed, as are the many styles of the Kissel. There are some seventy cars and trucks at the museum, including fire engines dating back generations. The museum is open Mondays through Saturdays 10:00 A.M. to 5:00 P.M. and Sundays noon to 5:00 P.M. from May 1 to the end of September. In the winter, the same hours are in force, but the facility is closed Mondays and Tuesdays. It is open for summer holidays but closed for winter holidays. Admission is $4.00 for adults; seniors (sixty-five-plus) and students (anybody who can show an ID regardless of age), $3.50. Kids from seven to twelve years of age are $1.00.

Kids who are into crafts will appreciate a stop at the **W.B. Place & Co.** leather shop, a factory outlet at 368 West Summer Street (414–673–3130 or 800–TAN–HIDE nationally). Leather made from deer- and cowhides are stacked in colorful profusion, ranging from purple to red to green, as well as the traditional—the result of various types of tanning practices and dyeing. Leather goods are also sold in the shop. Place is the place for both extensive and more personalized tanning processes. Local hunters regularly bring in their single deerhides for treatment, in addition to the more commercial aspects of the firm's operations. Get enough leather so the kids can make their own moccasins and Dad and Mom can outfit themselves in black leather motorcycle outfits.

The store is open year-round 9:00 A.M. to 5:30 P.M. weekdays, 9:00

A.M. to 4:00 P.M. Saturdays, and noon to 4:00 P.M. Sundays.

KENOSHA

The Wisconsin Information Center (414–857–7164), at the I–94 rest area just inside the Wisconsin border near Kenosha, is a great place to pull over for a breather and a pit stop. Plus the vacationer will find racks and racks of tourist literature, as well as knowledgeable staff behind the counter. For spur-of-the-moment side trips, or for added details on a planned getaway, the center can provide front-line help. It is open daily year-round 9:00 A.M. to 5:00 P.M.

Easily accessible off I–94 via State Highway 50, **Congo River Adventure Golf** challenges all duffers regardless of size or age. Waterfalls, deep pools, rock ledges, and jungles (all more or less real) provide a backdrop for a busy round of minigolf. But there aren't any hungry crocs, hippos, chest-thumping gorillas, or zebras to distract the concentrating golfer. The course is open seasonally from May to October, with summer hours from 10:00 A.M. to late evening. Call (414) 857–PUTT for all the details. Admission is charged.

Congo River can fill in the time for the older kids while parents do some preschool shopping at the **Factory Outlet Centre** next door, with its dozens of stores. The complex (414–857–7961) is open year-round 9:30 A.M. to 9:00 P.M. Mondays through Fridays, 9:30 A.M. to 9:30 P.M. Saturdays, and 10:00 A.M. to 6:00 P.M. Sundays. On Saturdays from the beginning of October to the Christmas holidays, the stores remain open until 8:00 P.M.

You won't find any bananas on the Congo River palms, but visitors to the Kenosha area will find plenty of fruits and vegetables to pick. A number of truck farms are open seasonally during the harvest. Such a family adventure can stock the home shelves with peas, pumpkins, beans, and berries, as well as provide a quality fun-in-the-sun outing. Here are a few places where kids can pick apples, strawberries, or other fresh goodies: **Munster Apple Orchard,** Old Highway 50, 1 mile west of New Munster (414–537–2664); **Oriole Springs Orchards,** 36116 128th Street, Twin Lakes (414–877–2436); **Smith Produce and Country Store,** 7150 Eighteenth Street, Kenosha (414–859–2645); **Szele Apple Orchards,**

11934 Twenty-eighth Avenue, Kenosha (414–694–8374); and **Thompson Strawberry Farms,** 14400 Seventy-fifth Street, Kenosha (414–857–2351). Smith Produce also has hayrides and carriage rides and a petting zoo. There is no charge for visiting the orchards. Call for harvest times when the best, new produce is out for sale.

Now for Kenosha itself. *Money Magazine* calls the city one of the best places to live in America for its location along Lake Michigan midway between Milwaukee and Chicago, its range of housing and accommodations, its business base, and all the cultural intangibles that contribute to quality of life. One of the best ways to see downtown Kenosha while taking a load off your feet is via the **Old Lakeshore Trolley,** which putters through the downtown business district. Weather permitting, the trolleys run from mid-May through Labor Day. Signage marks the stops. The trolley costs $1.50 for adults and 75 cents for children twelve and under. For more information on routes and times, call the Kenosha Area Tourism Corporation, (800) 654–7309.

Kenosha is not a small place, but tiny is really big at the **Miniature Village Dollhouses,** 1725 Fiftieth Street (414–656–0188 or 800–383–0188). With one of the Midwest's largest collections of dolls and their teensy homes, along with roofing, lighting fixtures, and lumber, the shop is an eye-opener for little girls and dads or moms who love to tinker. More than a hundred dollhouses are in stock, with a second level of the shop packed with Barbie items. Hours are 10:00 A.M. to 5:00 P.M. Mondays through Saturdays and 11:00 A.M. to 4:00 P.M. on Sundays. But call first on the weekends, just in case the folks there have taken a hiatus.

A stop to see the dollhouses means that the rest of the kids in the family who are not into dolls deserve a bag of malted milk balls from **Burke Chocolate Outlet,** 5000 Seventh Avenue (414–657–5000 or 800–472–7462). Ah, but Burke's double-dipped peanuts are the end of the world when it comes to melt-in-the-hand-as-well-as-the-mouth crunchables. Even the grumpiest high school heavyweight wrestler will agree that such a reward after the dollhouses is worth it. The outlet store is open from February to early autumn 9:30 A.M. to 4:30 P.M. It is best to phone ahead to confirm whether or not it is open.

For real thrills, take the gang on a tour of the **Stunt Education**

School, 10610 Burlington Road (414–859–2379), where trained staffers leap through fire, blow themselves up, toss themselves out windows, and generally tumble, fall, and flip around . . . just like in the movies. Call in advance to check times for visits, and warn the kids that under no circumstances should they ever try to do anything remotely similar to what these pros do for a living. There is a small admission charge.

Kenosha does have a more genteel side, to calm even the antics of the wildest little one by means of music from the **Kenosha Symphony Orchestra, Kenosha Pops Band, and Band of the Black Watch** (bagpipers can be genteel, really). For information about all the performing groups in Kenosha, contact the Kenosha Area Tourism Corporation, 800 Fifth Street, Kenosha 53140 (414–654–7307 or 800–654–7309). The folks there can provide times, dates, and ticket costs for concerts, plays, lectures, tours, and related artistic activities in the community.

LAKE GENEVA

Cruises on the 5,000-acre Lake Geneva have been a tradition for more than a century. Today's tours on the *Lady of the Lake* and other vessels range from one-hour to half-day jaunts, along with champagne brunches and lunch expeditions. **Geneva Lake Cruise Line** (414–248–6206 or 800–558–5911) can help with details. Kids will enjoy a morning cruise that features letter carriers who make flying leaps from moving boat to resort docks, carrying letters and packages to postal boxes. Between postal drops they tell about the estates on the shoreline. Seldom does anyone slip and plop into the water. But the way children are, kids always hope some postal person will get a summer's dunking. The mail runs sail forth from 9:45 A.M. to 12:15 P.M., mid-June to mid-September. The boats depart from the dock on Wrigley Drive, a block south of the main downtown intersection of Broad and Main streets. Ticket prices vary depending on the time of the cruise, but they are not more than $30 per person.

When one of the youngsters tells his or her brother or sister to "go fly a kite" over some real or perceived transgression, take the whole pack to **Aerial Stunt Kites,** 858 West Main Street, (414–249–0631). The high-tech operation makes delta wing kites via computer design, utilizing carbon graphite spears and Kevlar, spectra fiber, and spider line—all of which takes kite flying far beyond that of the dimestore variety. The shop also sells wind chimes, boomerangs, hammock chairs, lawn dice, tavern puzzles, and whirligigs. This is a hands-on place, where visitors are encouraged to try everything in the store. There is even an adult play area with jacks, marbles, sky tops, and pocket puzzles. So shunt the kids over to the brain teasers for a time so you can hunker down and shoot steelies. The shop is open 9:00 A.M. to 6:00 P.M. daily throughout the year, including Christmas and other holidays. Kite prices range from $29 to $200. Look for the latest playtime inventions, because many new toy devices are tested here before the major retail outlets put them on their shelves.

MENOMONEE FALLS

Two of the state's most easily accessible recreational trails launch out from this turn-of-the century community. The **Bug Line Trail** is a former railroad spur converted into a 10 1/2-mile pathway that is available for hikers, bikers, snowmobilers, and cross-country skiers. Pick up the Bug Line on Shady Lane in downtown Menomonee Falls, which is on the far northwest side of Milwaukee. The **Wild Rice Trail** is just over 2 miles long and is ideal for a scenic stroll along the Menomonee River, which eventually feeds into the Milwaukee River. Both trails are marked. And if that isn't enough walking for the kids, use a self-guided strolling tour of original historic buildings and take them on a tramp around the 1890s town. Pick up maps at the Chamber of Commerce and Industry office, W168 N8936 Appleton Avenue (414–251–2430), or the **Old Falls Village Museum,** N96 W15191 County Line Road (414–255–8343). The latter, open only between May and September, is a re-creation of the original Menomonee Falls and features a number of historic buildings that have been moved to the site. Be sure to call for hours, which vary. A small donation is requested. A gazebo there was built in 1980 by trade classes from local high schools, with design and funding provided by the Menonomee Falls Garden Club.

MILWAUKEE

The greater Milwaukee area is the largest urban concentration in the state, with almost one million people tucked between Lake Michigan and the outer suburbs. It is a party town, where something seems to be going on every minute—at least in the summer. This sometimes poses problems because of the subsequent scarcity of in-close hotel rooms. But never fear, there is always a place nearby in which to tuck in the kids. The Greater Milwaukee Convention & Visitors Bureau (GMCVB) is across the street from the convention complex called MECCA and kitty-corner from the Hyatt Hotel, just on the other side of the old Milwaukee Arena. The GMCVB, 510 West Kilbourn Street (414–273–7222 or 800–231–0903), is an excellent starting place to find out what is going on at any given moment, whether by phone or drop-in.

Also available with answers to questions about accommodations and goings-on in their suburban backyards are the Greater Brookfield Convention & Visitors Bureau, 405 North Calhoun Road, Suite 106 (414–789–0220 or 800–388–1835), and the Waukesha County Visitors Bureau, N14 W23777 Stone Ridge (414–524–8100 or 800–366–1961). The various bureaus are generally open year-round from 8:00 A.M. to 6:00 P.M. weekdays. From Memorial Day through Labor Day, the Milwaukee office is open seven days a week during those same hours.

Perhaps its greatest claim to fame is Milwaukee's City of Festivals image, rightfully earned. Check with the GMCVB for times, dates, and entertainment lineups. No matter the age, everyone in a family can find something exciting at Winterfest, Summerfest, or any of the ethnic festivals. In spite of frosty temperatures from December through February, **Winterfest** celebrates the season with snow carving, ice-skating in Cathedral Square downtown, musical entertainment, and restaurant specials. The square is opposite St. John's Cathedral, 802 North Jackson Street, on the lower East Side near the downtown business district.

But despite the claims that everyone loves winter, no one complains when June finally rolls around, with the **Scottish Highland Games** and the **Lakefront Festival of the Arts** (with its kids' art corner). So between sheepherding demonstrations by Border collies and the kilt-clad set, artsy wine and sculpture parties, the summer kickoff is a bang. The bagpipe bunch assembles at the beer garden and soccer fields adjacent to the Bavarian Inn (414–964–0300), 700 West Lexington Avenue, for a genuine multicultural experience. The arts festival sprawls across the Lake Michigan parkland directly north of the Milwaukee Art Museum, 750 North Lincoln Memorial Drive.

Most of the city's ethnic festivals, the giant Summerfest musical blast, and other outdoor activities are held at the Henry W. Maier Lakefront Festival Grounds. The 85-acre site is on Harbor Drive, south of the Milwaukee Art Museum where Chicago Avenue dead-ends. Drive any farther east on that street and you'll be swimming to Michigan. The park was named after a long-time mayor of Milwaukee who pushed development of the festivals.

Join in the polka dancing and enjoy the intricate folk dancing performed by Milwaukee and Chicago's finest Polish dance ensembles in their handmade costumes showcased at **Polish Fest,** the first major ethnic fest of the year, which runs for an entire weekend. Milwaukee's Polish restaurants serve up their mouthwatering *pierogi* and *smacznego.* Contemporary talent and top names in Polish-style polka music, such as Jimmie Mieszala and the Chicago Masters, get feet stomping. The annual egg-decorating extravaganza is always sure to bring out the Polish creativity in anyone, especially kids. For more information call (414) 529–2140.

For eleven days over the end of June and the July 4 weekend, **Summerfest** brings a wonderful range of music to Milwaukee. Summerfest is best during the day for parents with little kids because night-time crowds up with folks packing the dozen-plus stages to hear rock, blues, jazz, and mainline acts. There is a large play area in the center of the grounds, but although supervised it is not a babysitting service. Wheelchairs are available to rent on a first-come, first-served basis. So it is best to bring your own, if needed. Because of the crowds choose a designated meeting place at a certain time for the all-important parental check-up when teens are along. The information hotline for Summerfest is (414) 273–3378, while the general number is (414) 273–2680. The fest offices are located at 200 North Harbor Drive.

The **Great Circus Parade** (414–273–7877) rumbles through downtown in mid-July, bringing back the color and vibrancy of the good old days of the Big Top. The showgrounds on the lakefront can be toured for the several days prior to the parade. Dozens of authentic circus wagons can be seen and photographed; there are camel and elephant rides, circus performances and wandering clowns, plenty of cotton candy, and a petting zoo. It is a tradition for die-hard parade watchers to stake out sites overnight along the Wisconsin Avenue route and side streets on which the horses, acrobats, and bands will pass. Consequently, a first-time visitor may wish to purchase a hotel package from the Pfister, the Wyndham, or the Hyatt hotels; such a package usually includes reserved seating in front of the property and a lunch. The wagons are hauled to Milwaukee from the Circus World Museum in Baraboo, the former winter quarters for the Ringling Brothers Circus before it merged with Barnum & Bailey before the turn of the century.

The circus parade is held the same weekend as **Bastille Days** (414–223–7500) on Cathedral Square, where all things French come together. There is usually a voyageur encampment, fire-eaters, bowling ball jugglers, and an amazing line of Cajun, French-Canadian, zydeco, jazz, torch singing, and all manner of other sounds from several stages on the closed-off streets around the park. One entertainer has been returning for years. He tucks his bony frame into a 2-by-2-foot box and actually gets out again, to the amazement of onlookers.

Next is **Festa Italiana,** with fireworks and more fireworks, Italian food, Sicilian brass bands, a Venetian boat parade, and numerous entertainers singing "New York, New York." Festa prides itself on being a family reunion type of place. Naturally, guests get to munch pizza and all sorts of pasta possibilities. A religious procession through the lakefront festival grounds on the Sunday of the fest is great for the kids' photo opportunities. There is a special day for the elderly and another for the physically and mentally challenged. For details call the Italian Community Center, (414) 223–2180.

Then along comes **German Fest,** North America's largest authentic festival of German traditions. It begins at the end of July on Milwaukee's Lakefront. From yodeling to tuba playing, German Fest definitely taps the Old Country culture. Chewing on a succulent rib-eye and *spanferkel* sandwich, tour the traditional German town square, and browse in the marketplace for a new cuckoo clock or a colorful nutcracker. Dog lovers will howl over demonstrations by the Badger Dachshund Club and their famous speeding, ground-hugging Dachshund Derby, sponsored by Miller Brewing Company. For more information call (414) 464–9444. There are always plenty of lederhosen and polka bands, along with displays of Teutonic muscle autos such as the mighty Mercedes.

African World Festival follows, a celebration of African and African-American culture in the beginning of August on the lakefront show grounds. The opening ceremonies highlight rich African traditions whereby native priests bless the water and earth, accompanied by dancers, drummers, and singers. This authenticity continues throughout the festival. The motherland is re-created in an African Village and is also represented in the ancient dances, music, and fine African cuisine, which includes peanut soup and other exotic dishes. The children's area, featuring African storytelling, talent contests, mime, magic shows, and hands-on experiments, leaves children and adults alike with an unforgettable cultural experience. Rap, blues, jazz, and bebop are on tap from afternoon to late, late night. Vendors sell an amazing array of T-shirts, African and Caribbean crafts, records, and all sorts of other paraphernalia. For more information call (414) 347–0444.

The **Wisconsin State Fair** (with its hundred-year-plus grounds in suburban West Allis) pops up next for its eleven-day run, showcasing geese, horses, cheese, tractors, and geegaws. The best place to take a family, after watching the racing pigs, is the Family Center, where the Wisconsin Potato and Vegetable Growers Association serves up huge baked spuds, the honey folks have taste tests, 4-H kids dish out enormous ice-cream cones and sundaes (hint: the cherry topping is best), and the pork producers make sandwiches. This is eat on the cheap . . . and better for the cholesterol level than some of the fried foods found outfront on the midway. Call (414) 266–7000. It is wise to check with the fair office to confirm hours, as well as special discount days and other admission deals. The GMCVB can also provide details; call the number given above.

Then there's **Milwaukee Irish Fest,** the world's largest Irish music and cultural event. The fest emphasizes that it is a family affair, with an entire Castle McFest turned over to kids' activities. Youngsters can learn

Irish geography at the Lilliput minigolf range, designed in the shape of Ireland, with the holes the locations of major cities on the green island. Teachers direct arts and crafts activities that range from making potato people to fashioning Irish drums. Each year a play is commissioned for the children's stage (one of fourteen stages on the grounds). There is even a special category in the storyteller's contest for various age-groups of kids. And numerous troupes of young people dance, sing, and act. One of the most exciting presentations has been the regular appearance of the Trinity Irish Dance Company with various African-American groups, such as the Nefertari Dancers of North Division High School, demonstrating a delightful mix of cultures and percussion. Most of the major Irish and Irish-American entertainers in the world have peformed at the festival. Teens can really get into the Irish rock stage, with its showcase of rising young Irish talent. Once hooked on the music, they can then pick up the more traditional sounds. A Liturgy for Peace and Justice is held at 9:30 A.M. on the Sunday of the festival, with free admission via a donation of nonperishable foods that are given to area food pantries. An extensive program of classes in history, language, music, dance, theater, and related topics featuring lecturers from Ireland, Northern Ireland, Scotland, and other Celtic areas is held the week prior to the festival at the University of Wisconsin–Milwaukee. There are family package prices, as well as generally reasonable costs for individual sessions. Call 414–476–3312 for details.

Ola! Our neighbors to the South greet guests with open arms at the end of each August for **Mexican Fiesta** on the lakefront festival grounds. Musicians such as David Lee Garza and Elsa Garcia treat your ears, while burritos and tortillas treat your mouth. The El Baile dance competition, the El Grito contest, and the jalapeño eating contest all give people the chance to dance, shout, and, well . . . , shout for cash prizes. Car lovers will jump when they see the low-rider car-hopping competition. An unforgettable Mexican experience. For more information call (414) 383–7066.

Indian Summer in September, also at the lakefront, has colorful Native American dancers of all ages from around the country competing for top awards. But prior to opening to the public, the fest hosts schoolkids from throughout the metro area for a full day of educational events, with music, drama, discussions, and exhibitions on the environment and native culture. Subsequently, from the intricate footwork of the competition pow-wow to the competition for knowledge of tribal attributes in the Princess contest, Indian Summer is packed with Native American fun. Cultural and contemporary Indian performers entertain as visitors enjoy a juicy buffalo burger. Best of all, no one has to catch his or her own buffalo. More than sixty vendors display a wide array of Indian wares, while skilled native demonstrators share their handiwork. Get the kids up close while the craft-workers show off their intricate finger and basket weaving and the ancient skill of horsehair art. Walk through the four traditional tribal villages and soak in this rich heritage while looking over the various types of huts and tepees. The festival begins in the early half of September annually. For more information call (414) 774–7119.

The latest ethnic festival on Milwaukee's lakefront, **Asian Moon,** was launched in 1994, featuring music and foods from Chinese, Japanese, Hmong, Indian, Filipino, and other Far Eastern cultures. Dancers swirl with silk, songs touch on homelands, foods move far beyond the standard fried rice and into such delicacies as sweet banana egg rolls, *kung pao* chicken, and spicy pork with green beans. The fest is sponsored by the Wisconsin Organization for Asian Americans. For details call Summerfest at (414) 273–2680.

The **Holiday Folk Fair** in mid-November is a rainbow mix of all the ethnic traditions in the city, from Latvian to Serb, from Hungarian to Latino. Held in the MECCA complex downtown, Folk Fair is a food feast where you can turn the kids loose with a few dollars and they can come back to the table with six varieties of munchables, a dozen desserts, and plenty of change. A matinee on the Saturday and Sunday of Folk Fair presents youngsters performing traditional dances and songs, while evening shows feature major international entertainers and adult dance troupes. Many of the city's ethnic societies have stalls where they sell craft items, with plenty in the low cost range—perfect for kids looking for Christmas gifts for others in the family. Folk Fair, the oldest such program in the nation, is one of the major events sponsored each year by the International Institute of Wisconsin. Call (414) 225–6220.

Obviously, by the end of the year everyone in town is ready to curl up and doze.

But that isn't all on the calendar; over the year are many other annual events geared to families. Don't forget **Juneteenth Day** (celebrating the final liberation of slaves after the Civil War); **Rainbow Summer** on the grounds of the Performing Arts Center (a summer-long series of outdoor concerts, many of which are aimed at young people); **Maritime Days; Taste of Milwaukee;** the **Grape Lakes Food and Wine Festival; Al's Run** marathon; the **Rose Festival in** Whitnall Park; several Greek and Serbian festivals at outlying churches; **Sherman Park Blues & Family Festival;** the **Third Ward Block Party;** and numerous neighborhood street fairs and art shows offering plenty of exciting things for kids to do. Call the GMCVB for locations, hours, and admission costs (if any) of the different events. They are held throughout the city: from the lakefront to Inner City parks, from the north side of town to the far south.

It's enough to work up a thirst. When visiting Milwaukee, one of the first questions always asked is "Where are the breweries?" Although residents bemoan the title of Beer City, bestowed on it generations ago when a six-pack of America's largest breweries once held sway here, they know they can't kick a good thing. Although many of the eighty breweries that "made Milwaukee famous" in the good old days are gone the way of Schlitz, a victim of changing times, Miller, Pabst, Sprecher, and a couple of brew bars remain. Free tours are held at each plant, providing samples at the end of the educational walk—beer for parents and sodas for kids. There is, however, the sitting through the obligatory audiovisual programs on worts and hops. The tours are fun, though, involving some strolling, so be ready to point out sights to really little youngsters. They seem to be fascinated by the bottling and canning operations, with the whirring conveyor belts and all the clanking and clattering during the filling process.

Miller Brewing Company tours are from 10:00 A.M. to 3:30 P.M. Monday through Saturday from May through September, with fall and winter hours from October through April. The plant is located on the city's north side (Visitor's Center, 4251 West State Street), easily spotted via the huge billboards on top of buildings and roadway signage proclaiming IF

YOU'VE GOT THE TIME, WE'VE GOT THE TOUR. **Pabst Brewery** tours are offered daily year-round on the hour between 10:00 A.M. and 3:00 P.M., with Saturday tours 10:00 A.M. to 2:00 P.M. The old brewery complex is located at 915 East Juneau Avenue (414–223–6180), on the north side of downtown, just beyond the freeway spur leading to the Bradley Center arena and the convention complex. **Sprecher Brewing Co.,** 730 West Oregon Street (414–272–BEER), has tours at 1:00, 2:00, and 3:00 P.M. Saturdays only, with reservations required; however, its gift shop is open 10:00 A.M. to 6:00 P.M. Monday through Friday and 11:30 A.M. to 4:30 P.M. Sunday. Sprecher root beer, considered a gourmet soda by those who appreciate brown cows (root beer and vanilla ice cream), is so creamy that it usually leaves a delicious foam mustache on upper lips.

For walking (or driving) just to see the sights, secure the series of pamphlets on historic building tours prepared by the Department of City Development (414–286–5900). Each describes what to see and do in various neighborhoods around the city, from Juneautown to Bay View. This gives guests the chance to talk with locals, peek into tempting out-of-the-way restaurants, investigate mom-and-pop stores, and generally meet the community face to face.

Huge copper kettles transform simple ingredients into liquid gold at the Miller Brewing Company in Milwaukee. (Courtesy Miller Brewing Company)

A nautical way to check out the city skyline is via the *Iroquois* (414–332–4194), docked downtown on the Milwaukee River between the Michigan and Clybourn street bridges. Another cruise vessel is the *Celebration* (414–278–1113), which departs from 502 North Harbor Drive. Each boat offers on-board beverages, restrooms, and plenty of deck space on which to loll while admiring the lakeshore and harbor. It is especially fun for kids when the *Iroquois* heads out to the lake, causing a number of drawbridges to elevate as the vessel passes underneath after leaving its berth. Tell the kids it helps pick up steam to wave a lot at the folks on shore. Both vessels have well-informed crews who should be able to answer questions about the height of the Dan Hoan Bridge over the harbor, how many freighters visit the city during an average shipping season, and the depth of the Milwaukee River mouth. And no, there aren't any killer whales in Lake Michigan.

Call each cruise line to confirm its hours and excursion costs, which are determined by time of day, numbers in the group, and whether food is served. When the weather is bad and the water is wind-blown or too choppy, the trips are generally not offered. From late June through Labor Day, the *Iroquois* usually departs at 1:00 and 3:00 P.M. daily from the dock at East Clybourn Street. The *Celebration* has an impressive range of breakfast, lunch, dinner, and cocktail cruises between mid-May and the end of September. Prices are generally under $10 unless there is a meal.

Discovery World is a popular hands-on learning place for kids of all ages. Located in the central Public Library, 818 West Wisconsin Avenue (414–765–0777), it features displays that emphasize science, economics, and technology. Kids will be fascinated to learn how lightning discharges and how a laser can open an egg without breaking it. Discovery World interpreters are always on hand to help out. Visit Gizmo, the Scien-terrific Store, for educational games and science-oriented toys that help youngsters think as they play. It's all in good fun. Discovery World is open 9:00 A.M. to 5:00 P.M. Mondays through Saturdays and 11:00 A.M. to 5:00 P.M. Sundays. Admission is $4.00 for adults and $2.00 for students ages six through eighteen. Kids five years old and under are free.

And from the living, breathing animal viewpoint, there is always plenty to peruse at the **Milwaukee County Zoo,** 10001 West Blue Mound Road, (414–771–3040), with its exotic collection of critters. The zoo is open year-round. Winter hours are 9:00 A.M. to 4:30 P.M. daily from Labor Day to Memorial Day, with summer hours extending later in the day. Summer admission is $7.00 for adults and $5.00 for kids ages three to twelve; kids two and under are free. Winter rates are less. Parking is $5.00. Milwaukee County residents get a dollar discount for each admission.

The **Milwaukee Public Museum,** 800 West Wells Street (414–278–2702), brings together dinosaurs, the Streets of Old Milwaukee, Native Americans, African hunters, and a whole lot more. This is one of the country's premier natural-history museums, but probably the only one with a full-blown buffalo stampede on an upstairs floor (have the kids look for the rattlesnake). A return visit always opens up a new door to discovery, especially with all the traveling exhibits augmenting the core collection. Youngsters will come away knowing more about life in rain forests, tundra, and deserts than they ever thought possible. The museum is open daily 9:00 A.M. to 5:00 P.M. Admission is $5.50 for adults and $3.50 for kids ages four to twelve. Youngsters under four years of age are free. For Milwaukee County seniors and college students, admission is only $4.00. On Mondays, the facility is free to all county residents with identification.

America's Black Holocaust Museum, 2233 North Fourth Street (414–264–2500) is more somber, tracing the pattern of discrimination and race hatred in the United States. The displays are powerful and serious and point out the need to learn from mistakes. Kids need to be exposed to such exhibits so they help prevent such abuses in the future. Admission is $5.00 for adults and $2.50 for kids twelve and under. For groups of ten or more, tickets are half price. The museum is open 9:00 A.M. to 6:00 P.M. Mondays through Saturdays. Admission is by appointment only on Sundays and holidays.

There are more than twenty theater, dance, and musical companies in town, including the **First Stage** (414–273–7121), which gears its performances to children. The **Milwaukee Repertory Theater** (414–224–1761), **Skylight Opera** (414–271–8815), **Milwaukee Chamber Theater** (414–276–8842), **Florentine Opera** (414–291–5700), **Milwaukee Ballet** (414–643–7677), **Dance Circus** (414–328–3191), **Theatre X** (414–278–0555), and several ethnic theater companies (Irish, Native American, and African-American) are among those that keep the arts vibrant and alive. Kids can really get into the live performances, which are far and away better than becoming lost in the hotel television set. Teens have become fond of "poetry slams," in which readers compete for applause at local clubs. The **Cafe Melange** at the Hotel Wisconsin (414–271–4900) downtown is a top spot for this shades-of-the-beat-era. The hotel is located at 720 North Old World Third Street. And for more than twenty-five years, the **Coffee House,** in the lower level of Redeemer Lutheran Church at 631 North Nineteenth Street (414–744–FOLK), has had open stages in addition to regularly scheduled performers, offering a place where kids or grownups can test performances in front of live audiences.The shows usually begin at 8:30 P.M. Fridays and Saturdays, with an open stage at 7:30 P.M. Sundays. Tickets range from $1.00 to $3.00 but can be higher if a national act performs.

The flavor of Milwaukee can be captured on many fronts, from art to sports to activities to landscape. But the best, in the eyes of the backseat gang, is probably frozen custard. The city is known for its smooth, creamy custards served from stands dotting the city, many of which have been family-owned for several generations. Drive up the car to any one of a dozen stands (many of which look as if they date from the 1950s, which most do), unleash the munchkins, and march everyone up to the window to order a cone, shake, or sundae. Those who have earned a place on a personal honor roll of top-notch buttery custards includes **Gilles,** 7515 West Blue Mound Road (414–453–4875); **Leon's,** 3131 South Twenty-seventh Street (414–383–1784); and **Kopps,** 7631 West Layton Avenue (414–282–4080) and 5373 North Point Washington Road (414–961–2006). A good franchise operation headquartered in Milwaukee is **Boy Blue of America,** with outlets at 8322 West Lincoln (414–541–0420), 1681 South Sixteenth Street (414–671–5830), 6351 South Twentieth Street (414–761–2470), and 3928 South Seventy-sixth Street (414–327–1286). Yes, plenty of napkins are provided.

PORT WASHINGTON

The city of Port Washington has one of the finest harbors on the Great Lakes and is a center for the **charter-fishing** fleet in Wisconsin. Kids aboard can get the feel of being a Captain Ahab for a morning or afternoon experience on the

Big Water. Be sure they dress for the weather. A layered look is best because sweatshirts and jackets can be peeled off as the day warms up and the trout and salmon start flopping aboard. Among the top charter vessels using the Port as home are *Fishing Pox* (414–284–7222), *Foxy Lady* (414–258–0657), *Lighthouse* Charters (414–284–4484), *Nicky Boy* (414–284–9246), and *Night Flight* (414–242–4550). Call the various skippers to get the rates. Costs are usually under $300 for a full boat. Weather conditions determine sailing times, but expect to be up and out in the predawn hours for a morning charter. Call to determine afternoon departures.

Fishing has long been a tradition in Port Washington, charted in 1848, the same year that Wisconsin became a state. Subsequently, the **World's Largest One Day Outdoor Fish Fry** is celebrated the third Saturday of each July in honor of that heritage. Kids' games, fire department water fights, music, and lots of fish to munch make up the fun. A Fish Day 8-kilometer run kicks off the day's activities, with divisions for youngsters, as well as old-timer dashers. The Fish Fry is held in the city park along the lakefront downtown. Follow the crowds to the water's edge. Visitors can usually get a fantastic spread for under $6.00.

Winter certainly does not put the deep freeze on Port Washington. Cross-country excursions at nearby **Harrington Beach State Park** feature candlelight skiing, with ice-skating at **Kolbach Park** on East Whitefish Road and **Hill School Park,** at the corner of Grand and Spring streets (for details check in with the city rec department, 414–284–5881). Sledding is popular at **Hawthorne Hills Park** on State Highway 1, with snowmobiling at trails around town (for locales call 414–284–8259).

RACINE

The **Golden Rondelle Theater,** located at Fourteenth and Franklin streets (414–631–2154), was originally designed as the Johnson Wax Pavilion at the New York World's Fair in 1964 and 1965. More than five million persons there viewed the film *To Be Alive,* which won numerous awards from the likes of the New York Film Critics and an Oscar for best documentary short short subject in 1966. The theater was moved to Racine after the fair and rebuilt alongside the company's existing administration building, designed by Frank Lloyd Wright. Free thirty-minute tours of the theater and the Wright building are offered Tuesday through Friday and include the showing of one of several films, *On the Wing, Living Planet,* and *To Be Alive.* Kids will be amazed at the visual effects in each movie, with six-track wraparound sound and neck-craning giant screens. It is best to call ahead to confirm times because the theater is often used for corporate and community meetings.

Now here is a great activity for the "bravest" kids, ages seven to eleven years old. The **Racine Zoo Snooze** is held early each July, with a sleepout amid the lions and tigers. There is a scavenger hunt, a night walk around the zoo to watch nocturnal animals go about their business, a behind-the-scenes tour, an evening snack, and a breakfast. In mid-August the zoological gardens also holds its **Children's Zoo Debut** to introduce kids to the resident beasties. No petting, of course. Clowns, magicians, an animal show, and a silent auction with some animal artifacts are on the agenda. In October, the zoo holds its **Maze of Madness,** with goofy monsters and other spinetinglers in time for Halloween. For details on all these events, call the **Racine Zoological Gardens** at (414) 636–9189. The free zoo, located at 2131 North Main Street, is open 9:00 A.M. to 8:00 P.M. May through September and 9:00 A.M. to 4:30 P.M. October through April.

UNION GROVE

Plug your ears, hold on to your hats, and count to ten. The nitro-fueled jet autos at the **Great Lakes Dragway** make enough smoke, fire, and noise to rival a space shuttle launch. Hurtling down the paved runway at lip-cracking, nostril-expanding speed, the dragsters will amaze any kid into fast, faster, fastest. The track, on County Line Road on the east side outskirts of Union Grove, has attracted car lovers from around the world for more than two decades. Under the flamboyant baton of Broadway Bob, the outgoing, white-haired, fast-car fanatic who owns the place, the reputation of Great Lakes has been well earned. A walk around the back lot, where mechanics tinker on the cars and drivers talk warp factors, make it obvious that anyone into these tangarine- or hot-purple-colored land cruisers ain't into no Buicks. Many often have to use parachutes to slow down at the end of their run. Call (414) 462–5520 or 878–3783 for race times and details. Races are held from April through October.

WEST BEND

West Bend's annual **Germanfest,** held the last weekend in August since 1985, offers enough sauerbraten and *spanferkel* to satisfy the hungriest burgermeister and his flock. The southeastern Wisconsin city of 25,000 persons proudly shows off its Germanic heritage during the festival, which is just large enough to enjoy for a full day but small enough not to worry about becoming lost in the crowd. On the festival's Saturday a farmer's market opens before dawn, with tons of sweet corn and other fresh produce temptingly displayed from stalls and the backs of trucks. Call the West Bend Chamber of Commerce (414–338–2666) for details. The event is held throughout the downtown area with several streets blocked off and parking lots set aside for the fun.

Factory outlets for mom and dad are the rage here, with pocketbooks and billfolds sold at the **Amity Leather Factory** (State Highway 33 West, 414–338–6506), a range of wares at the **West Bend Factory Outlet Mall** (180 Island Avenue, 414–334–3477), clothing at **West Bend Woolen Mills** (on Washington Avenue along the Milwaukee River at Riverside Park, 1 block west of the Amity Outlet Store, 414–334–7052), and others with kitchen stuff, housewares, and appliances. The kids might not appreciate the time it takes to hunt out bargains, but when they receive a brand-new coin purse at Christmas, stuffed with dollar bills, the urchins should appreciate the earlier stopover. Then haul the tykes over to **Bierl's Cheese Mart and Factory,** 3721 County Highway P (414–677–3227) in nearby Jackson, for samples of award-winning baby Swiss. Or have the car full of cheeseheads try the creamy Muenster and brick. The shop is open Mondays through Fridays from 8:00 A.M. to 5:30 P.M., Saturdays from 8:00 A.M. to 4:00 P.M., and Sundays from 10:00 A.M. to 3:00 P.M.

Kids should take dad out on Father's Day to the **West Bend Rotary Seafood Fest,** with children's and dinner plates available. Seafood gumbo, shrimp, scallops, lobster (presold at $17.50 by ordering from the festival, 546 South Eighteenth Street, West Bend 53095), an oyster bar, plus smoked fish augment the usual brats, burgers, and corn-on-the-cob offerings. A hungry kid can be filled up for under $5.00. The pageant is held in Regner Park, at North Main and Silverbrook. Paddleboat rides, rock and roll, country music, face painting, line dancing, and tons of kids' games round out the family day. Call the chamber of commerce at the number above for details.

The city calls its 600 acres of parkland the Emerald Necklace, with hiking, ice rinks, swimming, tennis, bike/hike trails, basketball courts, ball-fields, and other outdoor amenities. Canoe launching on the Milwaukee River is permitted at Riverside Park, and there is a toboggan chute at Regner Park. But for inside folks, the **University of Wisconsin Center,** located at 400 University Drive (414–335–5200), features a fine arts series throughout the school year that brings in regional and national musicians and theater productions. The center's office is open 8:00 A.M. to 7:00 P.M. Mondays through Thursdays and from 8:00 A.M. to 4:00 P.M. Fridays. Call for times of events.

INFORMATION RESOURCES

The following are contacts to help families plan their best Wisconsin vacation ever. Start with the Wisconsin Division of Tourism, 123 West Washington Avenue, Box 7606, Madison 53707. For free travel literature call (800) 432–TRIP (outside Wisconsin) or (800) 373–2737 (in Wisconsin and neighboring states).

The state operates seven year-round tourist information centers for travelers. One is located in Chicago and another in Madison, while the others are located at major entry points into Wisconsin (Beloit, Hudson, Hurley, Kenosha, and La Crosse). Four other seasonal offices are in Genoa City, Prairie du Chien, Superior, and Grant County (at Highways 151/61, just north of the Highway 11 interchange).

Local tourism offices and chambers of commerce are also very helpful. They can answer questions, provide literature, and offer tips on what to see and do.

Here are several more valuable resources for information:

Association of Wisconsin Tourism Attractions
Box 467
Lake Delton 53940
(608) 253–6655

Golf Course Association of Wisconsin
Box 65
Mauston 53948
(608) 847–7968

State Historical Society of Wisconsin
816 State Street
Madison 53706
(608) 264–6428

Wisconsin Association of Campground Owners
Box 1770
Eau Claire 54702
(715) 839–9226

Wisconsin Department of Natural Resources
Bureau of Parks and Recreation
Box 7921
Madison 53707
(608) 266–2181

Wisconsin Innkeepers Association
509 West Wisconsin Avenue
Milwaukee 53203
(414) 271–2851

Wisconsin Restaurant Association
31 South Henry Street, Suite 300
Madison 53703
(608) 251–3663

GENERAL INDEX

ACTIVITIES INDEX

FISHING

GIFT SHOPS/SHOPPING

GOLF/MINIATURE GOLF

GROTTOS

HIKING

MUSIC

NATIVE AMERICAN RESERVATIONS/ CEREMONIALS/ MUSEUMS

PARKS

Trempealeau National Wildlife
   Refuge, Trempealeau, 104

WINERIES/VINEYARDS

Cedar Creek Winery, Cedarburg, 112
Spurgeon Vineyards and Winery,
   Highland, 89
Wine and Harvest Festival,
   Cedarburg, 112

WINTER FESTIVALS

Winter Festival, Cedarburg, 112
Winterfest, Milwaukee, 123

ZOOS/ANIMAL PRESERVES

Henry Vilas Zoo, Madison, 63–64
Irvine Park Zoo, Chippewa Falls, 38
Jim Peck's Wildwood, Minocqua, 48
J.R.'s Sportsman's Bar and Children's
   Zoo, Waupaca, 25–26
Milwaukee County Zoo, Milwaukee,
   131–32
Myrick Park Zoo, La Crosse, 92–93
Racine Zoological Gardens, Racine,
   135
Wisconsin Deer Park, Wisconsin
   Dells, 77

AUTHOR PROFILES

Martin Hintz, a member of the Society of American Travel Writers, has been a journalist for almost thirty years. He has written hundreds of articles about Wisconsin and authored Globe Pequot's *Wisconsin: Off the Beaten Path,* along with his oldest son, Dan. *Family Adventure Guide: Wisconsin* is in collaboration with son number 2: Stephen.

At the time of this writing, Steve is a sophomore at the University of North Carolina at Charlotte. Dan has moved on to his senior year in film studies at the University of Colorado at Boulder, after spending a year working in Venezuela. They do tend to get around.

Next in line is daughter, Kate, a junior at Pius High School in Milwaukee. Who knows? There might be a Globe Pequot book for her and her father in the future.

Hintz has authored twenty-five books and edited others for several publishers. His extensive travels have taken him to Chile, Hungary, Ireland, Finland, Canada, and throughout the United States. On many expeditions one or more of the family could come along. Stephen still talks about parasailing in the Bahamas when he and his dad visited there on an assignment for a newspaper.

But Wisconsin has always remained a primary love. After all, it is a family place.